Mitchell Coombes is Australia's most trusted spiritual medium and the best-selling author of *Sensing Spirit: Messages of love, hope and healing from the other side*, *Sensing Psychic: Amazing true stories of everyday psychic encounters*, and *Signs from Spirit: Inspiring true stories from the afterlife*. He is also the creator of the Psychic Soul Oracle Cards.

He writes a weekly advice column in *Woman's Day* and is well known from his countless national radio and television appearances including *Sunrise* and *The Morning Show*.

Mitchell has helped thousands of people worldwide from all walks of life through his extraordinary gift of mediumship, bringing them comfort and transforming lives.

To learn more about his work and schedule, visit Mitchell online at mitchellcoombes.com

Sensing Psychic

Sensing Psychic

Amazing true stories of everyday psychic encounters

Mitchell Coombes

brio BOOKS

All but a few names have been changed.

First published by Simon & Schuster (Australia) Pty Limited in 2012

Written by Mitchell Coombes with Denise Gibb

ISBN 978-1-922598-73-8 (print)
ISBN 978-1-925143-06-5 (digital)

Published in Australia and New Zealand by:

Brio Books, an imprint of Booktopia Group Ltd
Level 6, 1A Homebush Bay Drive, Rhodes NSW 2138
briobooks.com.au

MIX Paper from responsible sources FSC® C008194 www.fsc.org

The paper in this book is FSC® certified. FSC® promotes environmentally responsible, socially beneficial and economically viable management of the world's forests.

Printed and bound in Australia

Proudly Printed In Australia

booktopia.com.au

With appreciation to the Spirit World and
the wonderful people who have contributed
their heartfelt true-life stories to this book.

Contents

Introduction

The telephone rings. You rush to answer it. The person you have been thinking about says, 'Hello.'

For some inexplicable reason you feel compelled to take the long way home from work. Only later you discover a tragic accident would have blocked your usual route home.

Someone you haven't seen in years comes to mind. A few days later, you bump into him or her.

Everyone is naturally psychic.

Perhaps you regularly solve problems in your dreams – or experience 'ah-ha' moments out of the blue. Maybe your 'inner voice' guides the decisions you make. Or are you someone who *just knows* something without knowing *why* you know it?

Perhaps you can recall a time when you had a hunch and trusted it because it felt right. Have sensations like butterflies in your stomach or the hairs standing up on the back of your neck ever alerted you to danger? Maybe you've glimpsed the future, heard a voice from Beyond, or acted on an impulse that has saved your life. Every day, people from all walks of life sense the unspoken, read between the lines and experience events that defy logic. Subtle or dramatic, these are all hallmarks of natural psychic ability.

Within the following pages, I share with you remarkable real-life stories about extraordinary moments of psychic awakening. Astonished parents talk about the amazing psychic gifts of their young children. Pet lovers recall heart-breaking moments of saying goodbye to a much-loved pet – only to sense their welcomed return from the Spirit World days, months, or even years later.

These and many more heartfelt, surprising and profound psychic moments will give you the keys to open the doors for your very own psychic journey ...

CHAPTER 1

PSYCHIC POWERS

I was exiting the drive-through at my favourite take-away when I suddenly slammed on the brakes – spilling my drink all over the floor of the car. A teenaged girl, dressed in a white hospital gown, stood within centimetres of the bonnet. As she stared at me through the windscreen the name 'Elena' immediately came to mind. The girl's face was pale and drawn; her eyes were sunken; and her body looked like a hologram. She was very confused.

'Tell them to stop,' Elena pleaded with me. 'If they don't I can't go home with them.' And just like that, she vanished. I felt compelled to note the time – 8.00 p.m.

Two days later, Marcia, a 42-year-old mother of three, came for a reading. In my mind's eye I could see Marcia, along with a man and two younger children, keeping vigil around a hospital bed. They were crying. I sensed the family was saying goodbye to a much-loved daughter and sister.

As the reading progressed, Marcia's departed daughter's spirit came through. I instantly recognised her as Elena from the drive-through.

'Is your daughter's name Elena?' I asked.

Marcia nodded, choking back her tears.

Two nights earlier at 8.00 p.m. – precisely the time Elena appeared at the drive-through and then vanished before my eyes – Marcia and her husband had made the difficult decision to switch off their daughter's life-support machine.

'I feel so guilty,' said Marcia, dabbing at her tears with a tissue. 'I should have told Elena she wasn't coming home from hospital. I just know she's confused. She had no idea she was going to die.'

Marcia's intuitive feelings were right and my reading validated them for her. Her daughter Elena was confused, but the wonderful thing about being a psychic medium is that I was able to unite them one last time. Marcia asked me to explain to Elena how a sudden illness had taken her life. With that understanding came a great sense of peace. Elena crossed over, blissfully happy, leaving her mother with four simple words: 'I love you, Mum.'

Anyone who has ever received a message from Spirit is likely to tell you that it changed their life – as did my reading for Marcia.

For many, nothing is more profound than hearing their departed loved one is happy on the other side. Nothing comforts their heart more deeply than learning a departed loved one is still very much in touch with what is going on. Nothing heals their life more powerfully than receiving divine guidance and unmistakable validation that the soul lives on long after the physical body dies.

Every day my gifts of psychic seeing, hearing and feeling allow me to deliver much-needed messages of love, comfort and healing from the Spirit World; gifts for which I am truly grateful.

What many people don't realise is that everyone is psychic in their own unique way. Much like a mobile phone, some people are in close range and receive a full signal. Others are farther away and receive a weaker signal that drops in and out.

For some, the gift has carried through from childhood to adulthood, while for others, the gift may have faded only to resurface in their later years.

I started to see spirit people when I was just three years old – except I called them 'green people'. I would often wake in the dead of night to find their green human-like forms glowing at the end of my bed. The sight petrified me! There were nights when I ran screaming into my parents' room and took refuge in their bed. But with some gentle reassurance from Mum, I slowly began to realise the green people weren't out to hurt me. Mum said that if I listened they might even speak to me. And they did.

The green people chatted about who was moving house and who was going to have a baby – all the things a small child could understand and make sense of. Fortunately, my early predictions weren't put down to the wild imaginings of toddlerhood. I was raised in a psychic family – my mother and grandmother are psychic, as were my great-grandmother and her mother before her.

While other children played with cards, I read them. When I turned twelve, my Nanna Lucy presented me with my first deck of tarot cards. I felt so special because the deck she gave me once belonged to my Uncle Aram – an accomplished astrologer. I still have that deck of cards. I keep them wrapped in a special silk cloth because they are sacred to me.

Learning to read and interpret the various meanings of the tarot cards didn't happen overnight. I sense the same is true when developing psychic abilities. Much depends on the energies around you, the strength of your natural gifts and your willingness to develop them.

Four years ago, I arrived at friend's barbecue only to have him quickly usher me to one side. He asked if he could introduce me to Tony, a new friend of his who had an 'amazing psychic ability, but doesn't want to use it'.

I was fascinated because I couldn't imagine *not* using my gifts.

'I don't tell too many people this,' said Tony, after we'd been chatting for some time, 'but I see dead people all the time.'

'Do you talk to them?' I asked.

Tony shook his head. 'I try to ignore them, especially when they wake me up in the middle of the night.'

Tony and I laughed.

Listening to Tony's experiences reminded

me of my early years. Spirit used to wake me up at all hours of the night too! I explained to Tony all he needed was a simple sign to show Spirit when it was appropriate for them to communicate with him – much like a shopkeeper's 'open' or 'closed' sign on the front door. Many professional psychics refer to this as their psychic 'on-duty' or 'off-duty' sign.

'You could wear a particular shirt or pair of shoes – or even a piece of jewellery,' I suggested to Tony. 'That way Spirit will quickly learn when you're on duty and when you're not.' Creating psychic boundaries is important – as is a good night's sleep.

Enlightening and helping others, as Tony discovered by chatting to me, is just a small part of a psychic medium's duty of care. Much thought and consideration are also needed regarding the timing and delivery of spirit messages.

Once, while out grocery shopping, I heard a spirit's voice say, 'Mitchell, my wife is standing near you. She's really worried about our son. Would you mind letting her know everything will be okay?'

Only if the circumstances are right – and the person has given me their permission – do I pass on messages given to me this way. Psychic etiquette is very important to me.

Recently, I was browsing the shelves of a department store. All of a sudden I was pushed from behind. I stumbled into a woman browsing the shelves near me. You can imagine my embarrassment when I turned to see there was no plausible explanation for what had just happened. But as I was apologising and helping the woman gather her belongings, a little girl in Spirit appeared next to her. In that instant I felt the woman's overwhelming sense of heartbreak and guilt.

'Me bumping into you didn't happen by accident,' I said, smiling.

The woman tilted her head slightly as if to ask, 'How so?'

'I'm a psychic medium and I'm often asked to pass on messages from the Spirit World,' I said. 'I have a message for you if you're open to receiving it.'

The woman smiled a faint 'yes'.

'Do you have a little girl in Spirit?' I asked, gently.

The woman inhaled deeply. I gave her a moment to compose herself.

'Yes,' she answered.

'I feel your little girl passed suddenly – one minute she was with you and the next minute she was gone.'

The woman nodded.

'She's telling me to stop blaming yourself – does that make sense?'

The woman burst into tears. Tragically, her little girl was killed the day before her fourth birthday. She ran out onto the road straight in front of an oncoming car. There was nothing anyone could do.

'I have been in such a dark place,' said the

woman, fighting back tears. 'I had actually decided to end my life tonight.'

My eyes widened with alarm.

'But now –' she said. She halted mid-sentence before suddenly hugging me. 'Thank you so much. You have no idea how much you've helped me.'

In those precious few moments, the message I passed on from Spirit saved a woman's life. I felt hugely relieved that no harm would come to her in the future because her healing had finally begun.

I believe everything happens for a reason. Life is not a series of random haphazard events. There is a divine plan in place for each and every person – helping our soul to fulfil its destiny.

Some souls are on this earth to become great actors or artists, to find a cure for an incurable disease, or to bring peace to the world. Others are here to raise beautiful children, to create happy families and to bring joy to others. While my gift allows me to relay messages of comfort and healing from the Spirit World, yours may enrich your life in other ways.

Weeks before Maggie was scheduled for a reading with me she was taking a shower when she suddenly thought, 'Now is the right time to buy an investment property.' But instead of searching the internet, as she normally would, she felt compelled to take a drive and follow her intuition. Finding herself in an unfamiliar suburb, Maggie soon realised she was lost. So she parked near a street sign, typed the name into the street directory app on her phone, and waited. As if tapped on the shoulder, Maggie suddenly looked up. On the opposite side of the road was a house with a 'For Sale' sign out the front. Goosebumps prickled her skin as she felt herself fill with excitement.

Five weeks later, Maggie arrived for her reading. As she sat down she handed me a photograph. Without looking at it, I asked her to place it face down on the table and I closed my eyes.

'That's interesting,' I said to Maggie. 'Whatever is in that photograph is making me feel lost – like I'm not sure where I am. Does that make sense?' I opened my eyes.

Maggie smiled and nodded.

'Now I get ... Spirit is showing me a house that you're thinking of buying,' I went on.

Maggie grinned.

'But you already know it's the right house to buy – don't you?' I said, smiling. 'You sensed it when you first set eyes on it while sitting in your car lost and looking for directions.'

Maggie stared at me dumbfounded.

Psychic knowing can arrive as a fleeting snapshot of the future, a strong sense of knowing, or an 'ah-ha' moment in the shower such as Maggie experienced. How we experience divine moments of psychic knowing varies from person to person – just as it does from psychic to psychic.

A woman at one of my seminars once asked, 'Can you ever tune out from the Spirit World and turn off your abilities?' The short answer is no. In my life, Spirit World chatter is constant. It never stops. But what I can do is turn down the volume – just as you might do when the TV or radio interferes with your conversation or train of thought. Even though I might do that, I never stop listening. The instant I hear snippets of significant information or important messages, I immediately turn up the volume again.

Every week I drive from Newcastle to Sydney to appear live on Channel 7's *The Morning Show*. My journey is never tiresome or lonely because spirit people travel with me. One minute my rear-vision mirror shows an empty back seat and the next, someone is sitting there. I always say hello to my spirit passengers. Sometimes they just sit there, as if enjoying the ride, but most times they ask me to pass on a message.

Sometimes the messages are simple, 'You'll be reading for my daughter in a few hours. Tell her I like her new haircut?' Other times they're critically important, 'You'll meet my son David in a few days time. When you do, tell him not to sign the paperwork. All is not as it seems.'

Usually it's only a matter of days before I cross paths with the person for whom the message was intended, but sometimes it can be weeks or even years before I meet them.

Prior to a client's session, I often find their departed loved ones arriving ahead of time or waiting close by because they're so eager to pass on messages from the Spirit World. While this results in many happy reunions they sometimes let surprises slip without telling me.

I remember saying to one couple, 'Congratulations – that's great news about your pregnancy.' They both stared at me, replying, 'But we're not pregnant.'

'Well, you will be shortly,' I said, smiling.

The couple hugged each other. They'd just

finished IVF – it was their last chance at falling pregnant.

One lunchtime, I was mid-bite into a sandwich when a delivery man entered the front door to drop off a parcel. As I put my sandwich down and signed the delivery slip, Spirit whispered, *He's just been accepted into medical school.*

'You'll make a great doctor,' I said. 'You'll have an affinity with people because you know what it's like to be in their shoes.'

The delivery man dropped everything.

'I've told no one,' he said. 'How did you know?'

I pointed to the sign on my door and smiled.

Yet, just as Spirit shares the most wonderful news ahead of time, so too can they issue warnings.

A friend of mine rushed up to me brimming with excitement. She was busting to tell me where she and her fiancé had decided to travel for their honeymoon. Before she had even spoken one word, I saw a map of Japan. Alarm bells instantly went off in my head. I felt the ground shake under my feet. I saw my friend and her husband – along with thousands of others – washed away by a powerful wall of water.

'Please don't go to Japan,' I said. 'It won't be safe.'

My face turned white and my skin went cold and clammy. That was enough for my friend. She called the travel agent and cancelled their honeymoon booking there and then.

As it turns out, the day after my friend and her husband were due to arrive in Japan, a ferocious tsunami – spawned by one of the largest earthquakes ever recorded – slammed into the eastern coast, killing thousands of people. Hours later, dangerously high levels of nuclear radiation put many more thousands of lives at risk.

Profound moments of psychic sensing may come naturally in the form of feelings, inspired thoughts, dreams, symbols, pictures, and visions. While I often say my psychic abilities aren't about sensationalism, remarkable, surprising and sensational things *do* happen.

When you open the door on your own psychic ability, you'll discover messages from Spirit come to you in equally profound and astonishing ways.

CHAPTER 2

MESSAGES FROM THE SPIRIT WORLD

Lee woke startled. Something wasn't right. She glanced at the clock by her bedside. It read 2.30 a.m. She reached out in the darkness and softly laid her hand on her husband's shoulder. The gentle rise and fall the bedclothes suggested he was fast asleep. He was safe, but the gripping fear in Lee's stomach said someone in her home was not.

Lee slipped out of bed and raced to the nursery. She opened the door and flicked on the light. Her six-month-old baby daughter, Naomi, did not stir. As Lee leant over the cot and reached in to pick up her baby girl, fear gripped her heart. Baby Naomi was warm, but not breathing – and hadn't been for some time. Lee screamed – the pain of a mother's loss echoing off the nursery walls.

I met Lee six months after her tragic loss. Understandably, she was still adrift on a stormy sea of seemingly inconsolable grief. Lee's whole world had imploded that night. Losing a baby to SIDS (Sudden Infant Death Syndrome) is more than the human heart can endure. And even though I know that whenever a child passes, an angel is born, the pain is heartbreaking.

'Mitchell, I came to see you,' explained Lee, 'because I want to know if my visions are real or imaginary.'

In the broken days that followed baby Naomi's funeral, Lee continued to wake in the early hours of the morning. But each time she wasn't startled or fearful something was wrong. She could hear an angelic voice softly singing a lullaby: each time the loving, gentle sounds seemed to drift in from the nursery.

'I slipped out of bed and tiptoed down the corridor,' she said. 'When I gently pushed open the nursery door, a Heavenly figure – angelic, pure and white – stood with her back to me.'

When Lee stepped forward into the nursery, the figure turned around and smiled. Lee immediately recognised the angelic figure as her departed grandmother.

'I began to cry,' said Lee. 'Cradled in her arms was little Naomi – sound asleep and peaceful.'

Lee dabbed at the tears forming in her eyes with a tissue as she continued to recount her experience.

'Even though her lips didn't move I heard my grandmother say, "Don't worry, I'll care for her now."'

Spirit enters the lives of everyone, not just a gifted few. Sometimes their help is subtle; other times dramatic, but always memorable.

Christmas rose

One afternoon, just before Christmas, I was sitting with a dear friend of mine relaxing in her outdoor area. While she was savouring a glass of crisp white wine, I sipped on a refreshing mocktail.

'Mum was so good with roses,' said my friend, glancing across at the one potted rose bush she owned. 'But I've never been able to grow them like she did. I was hoping that one would flower in time for Christmas Day.'

By any rose gardener's standards, the buds on my friend's rose bush were simply too immature to flower, yet I sensed differently. A kind, reserved and nurturing presence stood nearby.

'I sense you should ask your mother for a rose on Christmas Day,' I said, smiling at my friend.

Less than forty-eight hours later, my friend stood at her kitchen window. As she rubbed sleep from her eyes she suddenly exclaimed,

'Oh my goodness! Merry Christmas to you too, Mum.'

Smiling back at her, from her one rose bush, was the most glorious single pink rose she'd ever seen.

Because they love me

Several months ago, while waiting in line at the bank, a sweet little girl stood quietly next to her mother. In one hand, she held a white feather – clutching it as if it were the most precious thing in the world.

'That's a lovely white feather you have there,' I said.

'I found it under my pillow,' replied the little girl, proudly.

At that point, the little girl's mother turned to see to whom her daughter was talking.

'Did Mummy put the feather under your pillow for being a good girl?' I asked, sensing that was not the case.

'No,' said the little girl, grinning, 'the angels did.'

'Angels sometimes leave me feathers too,' I said.

'Is that because they love you too?' she asked.

'Yes,' I said. 'Angels love everyone.'

Spirit will communicate with us using wondrously simple signs if we open our minds and listen with our hearts as children do.

Orchid miracle

Another friend of mine was moving house. In her garden was a prized collection of beautiful orchids. Thanks to her mother's green thumb, she'd kept the orchids alive for over fifteen years. Moving house without them was simply not an option.

Taking all the care in the world, my friend decided to place her orchids in a bigger, more decorative pot ready for transport to their new home. She even bought a top brand potting mix. But within days of having their feet in the new mix, her prized orchids began to wilt.

'Mitchell, the thought of losing them was like watching Mum pass away all over again,' said my friend.

With tears streaming from her eyes, my friend wrapped her arms around the orchid pot and said, 'If only Mum was here, she'd know what to do.'

That night, help arrived. My friend's mother appeared in her dream and said, 'It's the potting mix, darling. It's wrong.'

The next morning, my friend visited her local plant nursery and bought a specially prepared orchid potting mix. But the biggest surprise came when she went to empty the old potting mix. She discovered a fungus growing in the soil. Indeed, the initial potting mix she used was wrong – just as her mother said in the dream.

As my friend discovered, dreams are wonderful portals to the Spirit World – but so too are our five senses. They often announce the arrival of a spirit visitor.

Ringing in the ears

Not so long ago, I was only a few minutes into a reading when a faint sound from Spirit drifted in my left ear. As it gradually increased in volume, I realised it was the sound of a doorbell – as if someone in Spirit were holding their finger on the button. Curiously, the woman I was reading for began to rub her left ear.

'Is your ear all right?' I asked.

'I'm really worried about my hearing,' replied the woman. 'My left ear often gets a loud ringing sound in it. Today, it started the moment I stepped into your office for this reading.'

'Does the ringing sound like someone is holding their finger on a doorbell?' I asked.

'Yes,' answered my client, quite surprised.

'I sense the ringing in your ear is nothing to

worry about,' I reassured her. 'But I'm sensing there is a man in Spirit around you. He's two or three years older than you. Do you have a brother in Spirit?'

My client nodded. I smiled. 'Whenever you hear a doorbell ringing in your left ear – it's your brother visiting from the Spirit World,' I said. 'Invite him in. He can help.'

Like my client, many people discover they have at least one primary psychic sense they can develop. You may find you're strongly gifted in two or all three – psychic seeing, feeling, and hearing. Alternatively, you may find yourself inexplicably drawn to an object.

Take notice

For weeks Tracey, a client of mine, had been having silent conversations with her departed mother. She was trying to decide whether to seek spiritual healing. She was finding it hard to move on from a bad relationship. In the past, her mother had always given her such great advice.

'I was standing in front of the coffee shop keeping an eye out for my friend,' explained Tracey, 'when an irresistibly bright green flyer caught my attention. As I stepped closer to the public noticeboard it was pinned to, a gust of wind tore it away and plastered it right across my face.'

When Tracey peeled the green piece of paper away from her face she realised it was a flyer advertising spiritual healing sessions at a local healing centre.

'I think it was Mum telling me to stop procrastinating and seek spiritual healing,' chuckled Tracey.

Whenever you find yourself inexplicably drawn to a brochure, book, magazine or newspaper, take notice. Usually the content will answer your questions, point you in the right direction, or solve your problems. Lisa, however, discovered Spirit can also cause electrical disturbances to attract your attention and deliver a message.

Special blend

Lisa, a sole parent raising two small boys, once told me she had spent weeks worrying about how she could make ends meet financially. She'd been retrenched from her cleaning job and finding part-time employment within school hours was proving difficult.

'For weeks I'd been asking Spirit for help,' said Lisa, 'but nothing seemed to be happening.'

One night Lisa was sitting at her computer writing a job application when she heard a horrible loud noise – as if someone had switched on a vacuum behind her.

'I jumped off my chair then realised the horrible noise was the blender,' explained Lisa.

Alarmed one of her boys had woken up and was trying to make himself a midnight smoothie, Lisa ran to the kitchen. To her surprise, the kitchen was dark.

'The strange thing was,' said Lisa, 'the blender stopped the instant I turned the lights on. Only then did I realise it wasn't even plugged in.'

Then, just as Lisa switched off the kitchen light, the television in the lounge room switched on at full volume.

'A commercial was part way through,' explained Lisa. 'I picked up the remote to turn the television off when I froze in my tracks. The woman on the screen said, "I improved my income by retraining." I knew that was the answer I had been waiting for.'

Just like Lisa, many of my clients have also experienced their televisions turning on, radios bursting into song, computers receiving information while switched off, and CD players singing without a disc. When Spirit plays with electrical appliances it's their ingenious way of delivering a message, solving a problem, or giving guidance using the lyrics of a song, spoken phrases, or even advertisements. But as little Bree discovered, Spirit also possesses the amazing ability to make solid objects disappear.

Miss Money Shoes

'My youngest daughter, Bree, was only nine,' said Kath. 'One morning she woke up inconsolable. The silver sovereign coin her dad had given her before he died had mysteriously vanished.'

Kath swallowed hard. Talking about her husband was difficult even though it had been two years since he had passed.

'Bree and I turned the house upside down looking for her cherished silver sovereign,' Kath went on.

But as Kath was searching the house she suddenly thought, *I wonder if Bree is still thinking of her dad at night before she falls asleep*.

'Bree, honey,' Kath recalled saying to her daughter. 'Maybe Daddy is sending you a message to say he misses you talking to him every night.'

Bree promised to start talking to her dad more often at night.

'Two days later, Bree walked into the kitchen and said, "Look what I found, Mum."' She held up her cherished silver sovereign.

'Mitchell, my body bristled with excitement,' said Kath. 'When I asked Bree where she'd found the sovereign she answered, "In my shoe." I knew then it was an unmistakable sign from her father because he always called her Miss Money Shoes.'

Just as Bree's silver sovereign reappeared in her shoe to validate the fact that her departed father was still watching over her, Spirit can also validate their presence by making solid objects like flowers, feathers, jewellery, or coins seemingly appear out of thin air.

Pennies from Heaven

Margaret lost her son to leukaemia when he

was only twenty-two. On the first anniversary of his passing, Margaret wanted to be somewhere special – yet alone with her thoughts and memories. What better place for that than a quaint seaside café she and her son had frequented many times when he was alive?

'Mitchell, as I was seated at our usual table looking across the vast blue ocean I asked my son to send me a sign that he was okay,' explained Margaret.

Ten minutes later, the waiter placed Margaret's order down on the table. When she turned to look at her meal she couldn't believe her eyes.

'Resting on the table were three fifty-cent coins arranged in a pyramid, even though I had paid for my meal with a credit card,' said Margaret. 'My son always grouped his change in sets of three.'

Feeling a tingling sensation all over her body, Margaret picked up the coins. 'Mitchell, one fifty-cent piece was stamped with my birth year, the second with my son's birth year, and the third with the year of his passing,' said Margaret, incredulous.

As Margaret discovered, Spirit can bestow coins upon us or leave pennies from Heaven to mark a significant moment or date in our lives. But sometimes, Spirit will influence a chain of divine events designed to guide us in the right direction.

Divine collision

Jane was rushing to get to a much-anticipated date. She felt sure her boyfriend, Jackson, was 'the one' – her future husband. Pulling the hood attached to her jacket over her head, Jane shielded her face from the driving rain and stepped off the verge to cross the road. As she did, she rolled her ankle and collapsed onto the bitumen. An approaching motorist braked to a sudden halt.

'I burst into tears,' said Jane. 'There I was sitting on the road like a drowned rat. I'd nearly been run over and my ankle was so badly twisted I could hardly walk.'

As the male driver of the car was helping Jane to her feet, she noticed the last three numbers on his licence plate read *555*.

Concerned Jane's ankle needed an icepack, the driver insisted he escort her to a nearby pharmacy – despite Jane's loud protests that she would rather meet her date.

Five minutes later, Jane noticed she was hobbling into a chemist called Pharmacy 555.

'I told the driver to stop fussing,' said Jane. 'It's not like it was his fault he nearly ran me over.'

Nevertheless, the driver took Jane home. He even helped her up two flights of stairs to her apartment. Satisfied she was safe and could manage, he passed her his business card and bade her goodnight.

Five o'clock the next morning Jane woke. Her ankle was throbbing. She hobbled out of bed to the kitchen, poured a glass of water and swallowed two pain-relief tablets. She opened her laptop to Facebook her friends. As she did, the time and date leapt out at her. It was the fifth hour of the fifth day of the fifth month – five, five, five.

Jane rang me later that morning – curious as to why recurring sequences of the number five were suddenly tagging her life.

'Recurring sequences of the number five usually means buckle up because change is upon you,' I said. 'But I'm sensing there is one more set of fives to come.'

Jane burst into tears.

'Jackson dumped me by text message,' confessed Jane, between sobs.

'I'm sorry to hear that,' I said, 'but I don't feel he was ever meant to be "the one". I sense there is another man coming in around you who has left you three fives.'

'I'm not sure what you mean,' said Jane.

'The numbers could be in his address, phone number, licence plate, alarm code, sports locker combination – something like that,' I continued.

Jane was about to say she couldn't think of anyone, when she glanced down. Sitting on the table in front of her was a business card.

'I don't believe it,' said Jane, sniffing back her tears. 'The driver of the car – the one who nearly ran me over – the mobile phone number on his business card ends in five, five, five.'

'You'll be seeing a lot more of him,' I said, with a smile in my voice. 'He is a very kind, loving person – much nicer than Jackson.'

Just as Spirit can influence events and use divine timing to guide us in the right direction, so too can they reach out and touch us from Beyond.

Heavenly waltz

Teresa was worried about her 75-year-old mother, Joan, so she brought her to see me.

'Mum is doing the strangest things,' said Teresa. 'Since Dad's funeral she's been disappearing into the garden at the same time every morning.'

'Perhaps she is simply enjoying the morning sunshine,' I offered.

'That's just it, Mitchell,' said Teresa. 'I find Mum with her arms in the air, waltzing around my daisy bushes as if she and Dad were on the dance floor.'

I looked across at Joan. Her attention was elsewhere in the room – giving her an 'away with the fairies' look.

'Mum says Dad has come to collect her, but she's asked him for more time in the sunshine,' whispered Teresa, reaching for her mother's hand. 'I'm scared she is going to pass away.'

My eyes widened. What Teresa could not see was the presence of an elderly man in Spirit – one with whom Joan had shared a long, deep, loving soul connection.

'Your mum is not about to pass any time soon,' I said. 'Your dad is visiting from the Spirit World to take her dancing – that's all.'

'That's right, dear,' said Joan, suddenly joining the conversation. 'I can see your father. He kisses me on the forehead every morning before we dance in the sunshine.'

Teresa stared at us both in amazement.

While Joan sensed soft consoling kisses on her forehead from her departed husband, many others have experienced a firm reassuring hand on their shoulder or a comforting hug from Spirit.

How and when these beautiful things happen depends on what you've asked for during your quiet whisperings – 'I wish Mum could hear me', 'Send me a sign you're here' or 'If only I could see you one more time'. And, as Joan discovered, sometimes quiet whisperings go deeper into an awakening of psychic ability. For some people, talking to Spirit awakens nature.

Wings of hope

Catherine's grandmother passed one week before the opening of her new café. She was devastated. Catherine's grandmother was her inspiration and the driving force behind her passion and talent for cooking. Opening the café had been their dream.

'I was heartbroken Grandma didn't live to see opening day,' said Catherine, 'but the strangest thing happened.'

The night before the café's grand opening, Catherine whispered to her departed grandmother, 'I wish you could be with me tomorrow.'

The next day, as Catherine was about to cut the ceremonial ribbon she had tied across the cafe's doorway, a beautiful butterfly landed on the scissors. Not wanting to hurt the butterfly, Catherine gently encouraged it to move off the scissors and sit on her finger.

'Its feet felt like the soft touch of Grandma's hand,' said Catherine. 'So with a beautiful butterfly on one hand and pair of scissors in the other, I cut the ribbon.'

Once inside, Catherine welcomed her family, friends, and guests. While Catherine was proudly describing the choice of fabulous cakes she had made, the butterfly fluttered away – or so she thought.

'When I next turned to look at the cake cabinet, the beautiful butterfly was inside sitting on Grandma's decadent chocolate cake,' said Catherine. 'As I gently removed it from the cake cabinet, I sent a prayer of thanks to my beautiful grandma and asked for another sign.'

Much later when Catherine was serving her grandfather his tea and cake, the same butterfly was sitting on *his* hand – an unmistakable validation Catherine's grandmother was there on her special opening day.

Spirit synchronises with the natural behaviour of birds, animals and insects to deliver profound messages. Take note of the timing, because the chances are these happenings will be symbolic of events occurring in your life at that moment. I know in our family an owl is the bringer of wisdom and insight, often appearing just before significant family or world events.

Spike

'Spike is a rescue dog,' explained Marie, as we sat in a park watching Spike chase a ball. 'But I think he brought a ghost with him.'

'A ghost,' I repeated, surprised.

'Each afternoon Spike whimpers to be let outside at about three o'clock,' explained Marie. 'He then trots around the block as if being taken for a walk on an invisible lead.'

'I sense someone you were very close to once walked the block at the same time.'

'That's right – Mum did,' answered Marie, 'but she passed away over four years ago.'

'I also sense Spike sits outside one particular bedroom door and barks.'

Marie nodded.

'Was that your mother's room?' I asked.

Marie nodded again as she bent down to pat Spike, who had just dropped a ball at her feet.

'Spike hasn't brought a ghost into your house,' I said, reassuring Marie. I patted Spike. 'He's just helping your mother.'

'My mother?' said Marie curiously. 'What do you mean?'

'Well, Spike senses when your mother visits from the Spirit World and he's trying to let you know,' I explained.

Marie's mouth dropped open and then closed. I sensed Spike was a much-welcomed validation. There had been many times in the past where Marie thought she had sensed her departed mother's presence but had doubted herself.

Face in the clouds

'I didn't think I had a psychic bone in my body,' said Rowena, 'but one day, while I was planting spring bulbs, I had an overwhelming urge to look up at the sky. There looking at me was the face of my mother in the form of a fluffy white cloud.'

Goosebumps prickled Rowena's skin. It had been on her mind to visit her mum and apologise anyway. 'We'd had a minor falling out over the silliest thing,' she said, 'but as soon as I saw that cloud, I knew Mum needed me urgently.'

Rowena flew inside, grabbed her car keys and drove straight to her mother's house – paying no attention to the fact that she was still dressed in her gardening clothes and wearing muddy clogs. Urgency, mixed with an increasing sense of alarm, was compelling her to act quickly.

Fifteen minutes later, Rowena found her mother collapsed on the kitchen floor with the telephone in her hand. She had dialled all but the last digit of Rowena's home telephone number. Realising her mother had slipped into a diabetic coma, Rowena immediately called 000 – which ultimately saved her mother's life.

When we open our hearts and minds, we discover the Spirit World really does work in miraculous, wonderful and mysterious ways. And no one knows this better than very young children.

CHAPTER 3

PSYCHIC CHILDREN

'Mummy, the old lady who lives in the wall woke me up again.'

'Aunty Sue has something growing inside her that's making her sick.'

'You can't tell me off. I was your mum before I was born.'

Can you believe those profound statements were made by young children? I sense the unexpected and often startling revelations made by children are timely reminders that we too were once connected to the Spirit World in a similar way.

Millie

Two days before Janet was scheduled to meet with me, she raced into the grocery store in a screaming hurry. In tow and under protest was Millie, her four-year-old daughter. Millie had set her sights on visiting the toy aisle, but Janet didn't have time. She had lunch guests arriving in half an hour and had promised to serve her to-die-for prawn and avocado salad. The only trouble was Janet had forgotten an essential ingredient – avocados!

As Janet stood in the fresh produce section thumbing the tops of rock hard avocados desperately trying to find a softer ripe one, Millie tugged on the skirt of an elderly woman standing near her mum. The elderly woman looked down.

'The man with the funny-looking leg said "hello",' said Millie, with a bright smile.

The older woman gasped, steadied herself on her shopping trolley and then burst into tears. Janet looked up.

'Millie!' scolded Janet, before turning to the elderly woman. 'I'm so sorry: Millie thinks invisible people talk to her!'

The older woman drew in a deep breath.

'Sweetie,' she said, pausing to reach for Millie's little hand, 'my husband George did have a funny-looking leg – it was false.' The older woman straightened again and addressed Janet. 'Thank you,' she said, with humbling sincerity. 'You don't know how happy your little girl has made me.'

'I don't understand,' said Janet, watching the woman wipe tears from her eyes with a tissue she'd found in the depths of her handbag.

'George was the love of my life. He died four weeks ago.'

Janet gasped.

Perhaps you have a child like Millie? Maybe you know a child who has an imaginary friend or one who predicts events ahead of time. Many parents consult me expressing concerns about their child's 'odd' behaviour. Some even admit being frightened by their child's predictions or vivid past-life recollections. Others ask if it is at all possible their child can read their minds.

Naturally, many parents breathe a sigh of relief when I say all those behaviours are perfectly normal – young children are often natural windows to the Spirit World.

Windows to the Spirit World

Young children are incredibly sensitive and spontaneous. When they receive information from Spirit they react naturally – often with these moments of communication passing by adults unnoticed.

Happy birthday

Several months ago I was sitting at a café enjoying a hot chocolate and reading a magazine.

'Excuse me – but aren't you Mitchell Coombes?' asked a kind woman's voice from the table next to me.

I looked up, smiled and nodded yes.

'I'm very sorry to interrupt, but it must be fate that I ran into you today,' remarked the woman.

'Spirit works in mysterious ways,' I replied.

The woman laughed and introduced herself as Silvia. With her was her four-year-old grandson, Tyler.

'Mitchell,' said Silvia, lowering her voice as if she didn't want Tyler to hear. 'Can you tell me if the boy Tyler sees is real? Because it's causing all sorts of problems.'

'What sort of problems?' I asked.

'Two hours ago,' continued Silvia in a hushed voice, 'I was grocery shopping when Tyler suddenly blurted out, "Boy wants candle." He ran ahead of me only to return with a handful of birthday candles.'

'What did you do?' I asked.

'I explained it wasn't his birthday and told him to put the candles back. But Tyler stamped his feet and shouted, "Boy wants candle!"'

As Silvia continued describing Tyler's uncharacteristic behaviour, I began tuning into Spirit. A young man appeared beside her.

'Silvia,' I asked in a quiet voice, though one Tyler could hear. 'Who has the A sounding name – like Andy?'

Silvia thought for a moment. 'Well – there is my brother Andy, but he died when we were teenagers.'

'Boy wants candle,' chirped Tyler, looking up at me with a grin.

'That's right,' I said, smiling back at Tyler.

Silvia look confused. The penny hadn't quite dropped.

'I sense Andy is very much with you today,' I continued. 'And he says you've forgotten something.'

Suddenly, Silvia's face turned scarlet. 'Oh

my goodness!' she said, clamping her hand over her mouth.

'See?' said Tyler, with an even bigger grin on his face. 'Boy wants candle.'

Every year since her brother's passing, Silvia had never failed to light a candle and send a prayer to Andy on his birthday. This was the first year she had forgotten.

My heart reached out to Tyler. When I was his age a similar misunderstanding put me in a very awkward situation.

I was about five years old and it was my first day at kindergarten. After all the mums and dads had dropped off their children, hugged them goodbye and departed, one little girl would not settle. She just kept crying. So I walked up to her and asked, 'Why are you crying?'

The little girl answered with a tear-filled glare.

'You're really lucky,' I said, attempting to

comfort her. 'Your mummy is still here with you. She didn't have to go home like mine.'

Well, the little girl howled so hard she nearly brought down the roof. The teacher came running over to us.

'The boy,' she said, pointing at me, 'he's telling lies about my mummy.'

I couldn't understand what I'd done that was so wrong. Her mother was standing next to her as clear as day. It wasn't until sometime later that I learnt the little girl's mother had died four weeks earlier. To me, her mother looked as solid as the furniture in the classroom.

Very young children make perfect messengers for Spirit. Their arrival on earth is recent, so their minds are still pure. Not enough time has passed for them to adopt beliefs that close off their minds to the existence of the Spirit World. Doubt has no place in their thinking. In a child's world there is no such thing as a weird or quirky twist of fate, a stroke of luck, or a coincidence.

Lilly-Grace

I smiled, welcoming Olivia as she sat down in the chair opposite me.

'Mitchell,' said Olivia, passing me a delicate and ornate silver locket, 'I brought this hoping it would help with the reading.'

The beautiful locket felt warm against the palm of my hand. As I wrapped my fingers around it, I immediately sensed a huge wave of concern wash over me.

'Goodness me,' I said, giving myself a moment to recover. 'I'm sensing you have major concerns for your little girl at home.'

'That's right,' said Olivia. 'I'm really worried that Kate, my four-year-old, is fixated by her imaginary friend.'

'What sorts of things have been happening?' I asked.

'Lots of little things,' answered Olivia. 'When Kate goes to day care she insists I pack an extra play lunch for her friend, that an extra toothbrush is kept in our bathroom, and that I only read bedtime stories her friend likes.'

Olivia also explained that when she checks on Kate at night she often finds her sitting in bed giggling and holding out a toy – as if offering it to her imaginary friend.

'One time, I asked Kate who she chats to and she answered, "Locket girl",' explained Olivia. 'I have no idea who she's talking about. Mitchell, I'm really worried.'

As I continued tuning in, a child came through from Spirit and communicated *Mum* and then pointed to the locket I was holding in my hand.

'Olivia, I have a little child in Spirit with me,' I said, holding up her locket. 'She says you have a photo of her inside this locket.' Sure enough, hidden inside was a tiny photograph of a sweet little girl no more than three years old.

Olivia gasped loudly. 'Lilly-Grace is here?'

I nodded.

After Lilly-Grace lost her battle with

leukaemia Olivia and her husband vowed never to have another child. But as things sometimes happen, an unplanned pregnancy blessed them with little Kate.

'We've never told Kate about Lilly-Grace,' confessed Olivia, with tears in her eyes. 'We didn't want Kate to feel like she was the replacement child.'

'Well,' I said gently, 'Lilly-Grace is Kate's not-so-imaginary best friend.'

Silent tears of joy ran down Olivia's cheeks.

'Lilly-Grace says she helped you choose the pink fairy duvet you've hidden away for Kate's birthday.'

Olivia reached for a tissue.

Much too often out-of-the-blue utterances and the unusual comments young children make about what they feel, see or hear are dismissed as make-believe. And sometimes, when heavenly communications are innocently ignored or overlooked, Spirit has been known to resort to more unusual methods of communication – as Adriana discovered.

Ghost soldier

Eleven-year-old Kelly was convinced a ghost tapped on her bedroom wall at night. Initially Adriana, Kelly's mother, simply put it down to the little girl 'hearing things' – her mind was playing a trick on her. But after three weeks of Kelly screaming out every night, 'Can you hear it, Mum?' Adriana finally took notice. But no matter how hard Adriana listened, she couldn't hear the tapping noise.

Realising Kelly's problem was definitely out of the ordinary, Adriana decided the best thing to do was book a reading with me.

Once Adriana had settled herself down, I asked her if she had brought an item that I could hold onto. Adriana handed me Kelly's charm bracelet. Instantly, I sensed the presence of Kelly's so-called ghost.

'I'm being shown World War II,' I started,

'but – I also have a departed soldier coming through. He's tapping on my desk with his index finger.'

'Could that be the tapping noise Kelly has been hearing at night?' asked Adriana.

'Possibly,' I said. 'Did Kelly mention if there was a pattern to the tapping?'

'Definitely,' replied Adriana. 'It's the same rhythm and number of taps every time.'

'That makes sense,' I said, 'because I feel the soldier is tapping Morse code.'

Adriana looked surprised. 'Kelly's grandfather was taught Morse code during the war, 'but he's still very much alive.'

'I sense this soldier could be Kelly's grandfather's father,' I said. 'Perhaps you could ask him.'

Adriana's face fell with disappointment. 'Sadly, Kelly's grandfather doesn't know us any more,' she said. 'Alzheimer's disease has robbed him of his memory and we know very little about his parents.'

'I understand,' I said, 'but Spirit is telling me Kelly needs to visit him.'

'It's such a long drive to the nursing home, Mitchell,' confessed Adriana. 'We'll be wasting our time because he won't even know we're there.'

'You'll be surprised,' I said, comforting Adriana. 'I sense something unexpected will happen.'

One week later, Adriana rang me. 'Mitchell, we visited Kelly's grandfather – and you'll never guess what happened.'

Adriana said Kelly made several efforts to engage her grandfather in her intriguing tapping ghost story. Sadly, his mind seemed lost in the fog between the present and the past. But not willing to give up, Kelly grabbed two spoons and tapped a metallic Morse code on the wall – *dot dot dot, dash dash dot dot, dash dot dash dash*. In those fleeting moments, Kelly's grandfather's facial expression changed. His eyes lit up. In a clear voice he said the letters *S* - *O* - *N* followed by, 'My father taught me that. It was the first word I learnt in Morse code.'

'I was completely stunned,' said Adriana. 'The nurses had told me stories about Alzheimer's patients who fleetingly break through into the present, but I never thought I'd witness it.'

Kelly gave her grandfather a spontaneous hug and said, 'Well I guess my ghost is your dad saying, "Hello, son."'

Sadly, that was the last time Kelly saw her grandfather. I received word several months later that he passed peacefully just a few days after their visit..

If you sense a spirit visitor has entered your child's life, engage in the experience and listen without judgment. Ask friendly questions that show you're genuinely interested. Make the most of the opportunity you're being given to explore the messages, intriguing revelations, or incredible insights your child may be delivering. Who knows? You might be like Adriana and discover your child's spirit visitor is a departed loved one, or even more intriguing, an angel or spirit guide.

Angels and spirit guides

Before every child is born a guardian angel and several spirit guides are assigned to keep watch over them throughout their life journey. How each child encounters and responds to the presence of their angel and spirit guides is as individual as the children themselves.

'I was driving to the hospital,' said Alexandria. 'My father was dying from cancer. As I pulled into the car park my five-year-old son said, "Better hurry, Mum, Grandpa's angel can't wait much longer."'

Thanks to her son, Alexandria made it to the ward just in time to hold her father's hand and tell him she loved him before he closed his eyes for the final time.

'My five-year-old daughter looked up at

me one day and whispered, "My fairy godmother said Uncle Tom's brakes are broken,"' explained Emily. 'The next day, my brother Tom rang to say his brakes had failed and that he'd written off his car.'

I sense angels and spirit guides are like teachers. They guide and mentor children while they're in earth's classroom with timely messages, healing remedies and, in some cases, by intervening with life-saving measures – as Lucy discovered.

Wake up

Late one night, Lucy was driving home from her mother's home in the country. In the back, secured in his booster seat, was her fourteen-month-old son, Nathan.

'Halfway home I remember feeling tired,' said Lucy. 'Next thing – I felt baby Nathan yank my hair so hard I screamed.'

Startled awake by her own scream, Lucy

snapped open her eyes – instantly realising she'd fallen asleep at the wheel.

Turning the steering wheel sharply, the tyres squealed as they struggled to hold the car on the road. 'One second later,' recalled Lucy, 'it would have been too late.' Her car would have plummeted down a steep ravine.

Shaken by her near-miss, Lucy pulled over. Trembling all over, she turned to look back at baby Nathan in the rear seat. He kicked his legs and giggled.

How did you manage to pull my hair? Lucy recalled thinking to herself.

Stepping out of the car, Lucy opened the rear passenger door and unbuckled Nathan from his booster seat. Just as she was about to pick him up and hug him for dear life, he giggled and pointed.

'Angel,' he said very clearly, looking to a point over Lucy's shoulder.

Shortly after her traumatic journey, Lucy booked a reading with me. 'Was my experience real?' she asked. 'Did my son's angel really intervene to save us both?' My answers were 'yes' and 'yes'.

Lucy's story is just one of many miraculous life-saving interventions I hear about nearly every day.

Dolly get hurt

The night before Justine and her husband John flew out to Bali their three-year-old daughter Eve ran into their bedroom crying, 'Dolly no go to Bali.'

When Justine asked why, Eve replied, 'Dolly get hurt.'

For several months little Eve had been speaking about 'Dolly'. 'Dolly no do that', 'Dolly like this one better' and 'Dolly's favourite colour is blue'. John and Justine thought 'Dolly' was simply an imaginary friend. However, they also noticed that Dolly was also responsible for most of Eve's misdoings.

On the morning the taxi arrived to drive

them all to the airport Justine checked her handbag one last time. Within easy reach were their passports, but not the airline tickets. They had suddenly vanished.

'Does Dolly have our tickets?' asked Justine, looking directly at Eve.

Yes, nodded Eve.

'Where did Dolly hide our tickets?' asked Justine, masking her panic.

'Dolly said no go,' responded Eve, shaking her head defiantly.

Twenty frustrating minutes later, Justine managed to locate where Eve had hidden the tickets. They arrived at the departure gate with less than five minutes to spare.

A few hours later, Justine, John and Eve touched down in beautiful Bali. They cleared customs with little fuss, hailed a taxi, and headed toward their hotel in Kuta. They were finally on holiday in paradise.

Two days later, John woke complaining of a sore throat and feverish chills. When Justine felt his forehead it was obvious he was running a raging temperature. Justine gave him two paracetamol tablets, made sure the room was cool, and instructed John to rest in bed.

'With John ill,' said Justine, 'I decided to take Eve shopping at Kuta Square Mall.'

But once Justine arrived at the shopping mall, Eve became increasingly agitated. She kept refusing to go into shops and would just pull on Justine's hand saying, 'Dolly no like'.

'Eve became so irritable,' said Justine, 'I gave up trying to shop and decided to walk back to the hotel.'

Toward dinner time, John was still feverish and not well enough to venture out. So Justine decided to walk back to her favourite restaurant near the Kuta Square Mall and buy dinner. Her plan was to return to their hotel room and eat it with John. But just as she was about to step through the doorway of Raja's Restaurant Eve let out a blood-curdling scream.

Eve broke free from Justine and ran like the

wind into the crowded, dimly lit street. Justine gave chase, but Eve wove her way between the masses of jostling tourists with alarming skill.

'I didn't catch up with her until we were almost back at the hotel,' explained Justine. 'And just as I scooped Eve off the ground and saddled her on my hip I heard a massive explosion.'

The ground underneath Justine's feet vibrated and the repercussion from the blast rattled the hotel windows above her. Seconds later, another sickening explosion caused Justine to drop to her knees and shield Eve with her own body.

The date was 12 October 2002. Miraculously, Justine and Eve had narrowly escaped being among the 202 innocent victims killed by two horrific bomb blasts – the worst act of terrorism in Bali to date.

From that day on, 'Dolly' was no longer Eve's imaginary friend. For Justine and John, 'Dolly' was their saviour.

Young children often don't recognise the identity or significance of their angels or spirit guides when they first appear. Even at the age of seven, I was still insisting that Mum set an extra place at the dinner table for my spirit friend.

Many parents worry that an imaginary friend marks the beginning of a mental health problem, or that their child is lonely or isolated. In most cases, nothing could be further from the truth. In my experience, an imaginary friend who remains a constant companion usually turns out to be a spirit guide. I know mine did.

Like teachers, angels and spirit guides watch over and mentor our children using all forms of miraculous communication, but every so often a child is born into earth's classroom who is a divine teacher.

Angel hearts

For months my friend's seven-year-old daughter, Kelly, had been collecting old greeting cards.

One day, my friend arrived home from work. Spread out on the kitchen table were dozens of beautiful decoupage heart shapes – each with a pink ribbon threaded through the top. Before my friend could ask her daughter why she had made so many, she heard Kelly say, 'Bless these hearts with healing.'

'What are you doing?' asked my friend, finally making her presence known to her daughter.

'Making angel hearts,' answered Kelly.

'Why?' asked my friend.

'My angel said I could help all the sick children in hospital by giving them angel heart healing.'

I call children who naturally offer healing, bring people together, or deliver profound messages beyond their years, *teacher souls*.

Teacher souls radiate joy and love. They unite families, give unconditional love and bring great healing to all those who cross their path. My friend's daughter is a teacher soul whom I'm sure will bring healing to many throughout the course of her life.

Children who have lived before

Has your child ever surprised you with vivid recollections from a past life? Many young children spontaneously recall memories from their previous lifetimes without any kind of prompting.

Perhaps you've been on the receiving end of comments like, 'I remember when I was the parent and *you* were the child' or 'I died before you were born'.

Much of what young children remember about their past life is astounding. And the ways in which they recall specific details is simply remarkable.

Picture-book mum

'I remember when my daughter, Alexis, had just turned five,' said Sandra. 'She was sitting on the floor colouring in when she stopped, looked up at me and said, "I remember when I picked you from a book." '

'What do you mean?' asked Sandra.

'The big book – the one with all the mums and dads in it.'

'I don't think I know that book,' said Sandra.

'It's only for before you're born,' explained Alexis. 'I picked you because I liked your curly red hair.'

'What about Daddy?' asked Sandra.

'He looked strong. I knew he could whiz me around in the air.'

Sandra's story reminds me of another client. Her four-year-old son was sitting quietly with his dad on their couch. Part way through a documentary about Japan's super-fast train system, my client's son turned to his dad and said, 'I drived a train once.'

'But you haven't been to Japan,' responded my client's husband.

'Not in Japan, silly. Here – before you were born – when they puffed out steam.'

Another similar, yet very famous past life recollection is that of American-born James Leininger. He was just two years old when he started screaming out in the middle of the night, 'Airplane crash! Plane on fire! Little man can't get out!'

As James grew older it became very clear that information coming from his 'crash-and-burn' fighter pilot nightmares, spontaneous utterances, and war plane drawings demonstrated an astonishing historical knowledge well beyond his years.

Four years later, at the age of six, it was proven beyond a shadow of a doubt that James Leininger was actually recalling his past life. He once was Lieutenant James McCready Huston Junior, a World War II fighter pilot who died in

1945 at the age of twenty-one. James's story is remarkable and much detailed online.

I have long said that the spontaneous past-life recollections of children offer the best evidence yet for reincarnation. Now it seems science agrees. All over the world children's past-life memories are being 'scientifically' documented. Yet, perhaps the most important point of all is that these stories validate there is life after death; that our souls do live on; and that we've all had more than one life.

Gibberish

'When Cooper was nearly five I checked in on him early one morning and discovered he had a raging fever,' said Raeleen. 'As I placed the digital thermometer in his ear he looked up at me with his sunken eyes and pale little face and said, "Mi gira la testa." '

Frightened by Cooper's delirium – he was speaking gibberish – Raeleen rushed him straight to the emergency department of the nearest children's hospital.

'As I was comforting Cooper he looked up at the nurse assessing him and said "Ho la nausea",' explained Raeleen.

But just as Raeleen was about apologise for Cooper's fever-driven gibberish the nurse exclaimed, 'Gosh, Cooper – you speak Italian, just like me.'

Thanks to the nurse, Raeleen discovered that 'Mi gira la testa' and 'Ho la nausea' are Italian for 'I feel dizzy' and 'I feel sick'.

'Mitchell, I was totally stunned,' confessed Raeleen. 'I had no idea where or when Cooper learnt to speak Italian words and phrases.'

As it turns out, Cooper wasn't only speaking smatterings of Italian. He often complained he disliked the cold weather in Canberra – that he much preferred life when he lived once before. 'In Italy,' Raeleen recalled Cooper saying, 'the weather was warmer, I was a dad and I grew vegetables.'

While some children have been known to recall foreign words or phrases from a past life, others draw pictures or relive past-life experiences in their dreams. For many children, past-life recollections vary from vivid and detailed accounts through to fleeting snippets – like recalling their name from a previous lifetime.

I know one little five-year-old girl who startled her mother and two aunts with her past-life recollection. She suddenly interrupted their afternoon tea and announced, 'I was a French chorus dancer.' When her mum and aunts laughed, she performed an impromptu and near perfect cancan. They were left speechless.

Could past-life experiences explain why some children are born with passionate interests that reach well beyond their years, fears that go well beyond their experiences, and knowledge that far outreaches their learning? I believe so.

If you suspect your child is having past-life

recollections, ask questions that clarify any details you don't understand. Be sure to include questions like, 'What was your name before?', 'What did you do for work?', 'What were your favourite things?' and 'What clothes did you wear?'. Questions like these provide a wonderful framework in which to explore a child's past-life recollections.

By asking questions and keeping an open mind, you might even learn something about yourself. After all, many children turn out to be wise old souls with more than one lifetime's worth of lessons tucked under their belts.

CHAPTER 4

PSYCHIC PETS

A question I'm often asked is, 'Are pets naturally psychic?'

I sense that just like children, our pets are more open to the psychic signals they receive because their minds aren't conditioned by limited teachings or narrowed by rigid views of the world. Our pets simply express their feelings and behave in the only way they know how when they receive information through their psychic antenna.

Dexter

Doug, a gentleman in his late fifties, sat in front of me.

'I've never done this sort of thing before,' he said, fidgeting.

Despite his nervousness, Doug hoped to make a connection with a departed loved one, whom he missed dearly.

'I have a kind and gentle lady here,' I said to Doug. 'She's telling me her name is June.'

'That's my wife,' responded Doug.

Just as I felt Doug relax, June stepped aside and the presence of lovable but huge animal burst through from Spirit.

'Goodness gracious,' I said. 'I sense there is an enormous dog with her.'

Doug was speechless.

'Now June is laughing,' I said. 'She is saying this dog belongs to you.'

'June has Dexter?' asked Doug, smiling.

'Yes,' I said.

Doug grinned. 'Dexter was my Rottweiler,' he said with pride.

'June says she was greeted by Dexter when she passed – he helped her cross over into the Spirit World,' I added.

Silent tears began to roll down Doug's cheeks. I paused for a moment.

'Your wife also tells me there was something special about Dexter, besides his enormous size.'

Doug pulled a handkerchief from his shirt pocket and dabbed at his tears. 'I used to joke with June that Dexter was psychic.'

I was intrigued.

'Dexter could hear me call him in my thoughts,' Doug said.

At first, June laughed off the idea that Dexter had psychic powers. She even lovingly accused Doug of bribing Dexter with his favourite treats – Schmackos. But time after time Doug proved her wrong. Dexter really did know when Doug was silently calling him.

'Once, I got my hand caught in a piece of machinery,' continued Doug. 'Although Dexter was elsewhere, I willed him to bring help – and he did.'

Whenever Doug was out, Dexter would walk himself to the garage and sit by the door exactly fifteen minutes before his master's arrival home – irrespective of how long Doug had been away.

'One night, Dexter started howling for no reason at all,' said Doug. 'He was howling for a good half-hour before the phone rang. When it did, Dexter stopped immediately. He tilted his head to one side and stared at my face in intense silence. The caller told me my only son had just been involved in a serious car accident and was in a critical condition.'

Understandably, Doug was in a state of shock and reached for the closest chair. Within an instant, Dexter was at Doug's side. He rested his chin on Doug's thigh in an effort to comfort him.

'I'm being shown Dexter passed three years before your wife – does that make sense?' I asked.

'Yes,' answered Doug, with an air of great sadness in his voice. 'June found Dexter frothing at the mouth. She rushed him to the vet and then rang me, but I couldn't leave work in time to visit him.'

Doug told me he awoke early the next morning distressed and panicked. Dexter was calling him in his dreams.

'I didn't think twice. I just jumped in my car and drove like a madman to the vet hospital,' said Doug.

The night watchman found Doug rattling at the front doors of the hospital. Doug tried to explain Dexter was inside, very sick, and was calling him. But the night watchman took one look at Doug, still dressed in his pyjamas, and told him to go home.

Tears welled up in Doug's eyes again. 'I knew it wasn't good, Mitchell. For the first time ever,

Dexter had called out to me for help and I had let him down,' said Doug.

Seven-thirty that morning, the phone rang. It was the vet. Sadly, Dexter had passed during the night.

'Well, Doug,' I said. 'Dexter is with June and she says he wasn't calling to you to rescue him that night.'

'He wasn't?'

'No. June says Dexter is safe and happy – you don't need to feel guilty any more.'

Doug stared at me in disbelief. Then, ever so slowly, I felt the burden of guilt lift from his shoulders. I knew he finally had the closure he needed.

I have known many departed pets to appear during readings. With tails wagging, coats shining, and feathers fluffing, pets charge through from the Spirit World with much enthusiasm. Some arrive with messages while others are simply offering their affection once again.

A pet's devotion becomes an unbreakable bond – one that will compel them to make long, arduous journeys home. After all, home is where pets are petted, stroked and loved. Kids play with them and everyone in the household knows their favourite foods, toys and places to curl up and go to sleep.

Ruby

One Christmas morning, a client of mine received the best present in the world. She opened the front door to find her long-lost Labrador, Ruby, sitting on her front steps.

'I don't believe it,' she said. 'Ruby?'

Ruby looked up at the sound of her owner's voice and barked once before limping inside, wagging her tail.

'We lost Ruby in 2008,' explained my client. 'We'd just moved towns and I let Ruby out for a run, but she never came home.'

My client searched for over twelve months

before finally resigning herself to the fact that Ruby was never coming back.

Another client of mine, Tammy, suffered a bitter divorce. After dividing the assets and resolving other financial issues, Tammy's ex-husband, Scott, stooped to his deepest low: he insisted Trixie, Tammy's beloved cat, live with him. Even though Scott didn't have an ounce of compassion for Trixie, he knew taking her would be as cruel as wrenching a baby out of Tammy's arms.

After the divorce Tammy was heartbroken. Her life was shattered. Not only was she forced to move to a new suburb over twenty kilometres away but she had to live without Trixie. Tammy felt betrayed, tired and broken. Then one sunny day, six months later, a beautiful tortoiseshell cat jumped up and landed on Tammy's kitchen window ledge.

'Meow,' cried a familiar feline voice.

Tammy stopped washing her dishes, looked

up from the kitchen sink and burst into tears of joy.

'I don't know how she did it, Mitchell, but Trixie found me.'

Not only will pets make difficult journeys to be reunited with their families but their love will transcend the tests of time, distance, and even death – as Jenny discovered.

Angel the cat

The July afternoon had turned cold and windy. Jenny walked into my office folding her umbrella. As I waited for her to slip the wet umbrella into its cover I sensed the spirit of a departed pet alongside her. Yet when Jenny sat down she said, 'Love, money, work and future,' and then handed me her wedding ring.

It was obvious to me Jenny wasn't expecting a message from a departed pet. But as I closed my eyes and wrapped my hand tight around the ornate gold band, an enormous wave of love, devotion and loyalty swept over me.

'I am sensing the most amazing, adorable, loving presence here with us, and I believe it's a cat. Does that make sense?' I asked.

Jenny's mouth opened but no words came out.

'Yes, it's definitely a cat,' I confirmed. 'She's the sweetest little thing and she definitely belongs to you.'

Jenny immediately rummaged through her handbag. 'Do you mean this one?' she asked, handing me a photo of a cat.

'Yes,' I said. 'That's her.'

'That's my little Angel,' said Jenny.

I soon learnt Jenny had rescued Angel from a gutter. When Jenny found Angel she was abandoned, sick and near death. Yet when Jenny lifted her tiny body out of the gutter something about her knotted white fur, pink nose, and pert whiskers melted Jenny's heart.

'She had the sweetest face and cutest paws,' said Jenny. 'She looked like she'd just padded through grey paint.'

When Jenny arrived home with the abandoned kitten, her two daughters had the same instant reaction. It was love at first sight.

Right away, Jenny's daughters riffled through her best shoes to find a shoebox to make Angel a bed. Jenny was so proud of her daughters' inventiveness. They even lined the shoebox with soft cotton padding. Jenny's daughters did everything to keep Angel's feeble little body safe and warm. But Jenny could tell Angel's life was hanging in the balance. Wasting no time, Jenny rushed Angel to her trusted local vet.

The vet peered into the shoebox and gently raised Angel's limp body to his eye level. She let out a faint 'meow' that was more like a squeak. The vet turned her body this way and that before shaking his head.

'She's too far gone,' Jenny recalled the vet saying. 'There's little hope of saving her.'

Angel looked at Jenny and gave another faint 'meow' that was barely audible above the vet's voice. Jenny closed her eyes and took in a deep breath while processing the vet's words. Jenny felt sure there was something about Angel that was worth fighting for. Hope was not lost.

'I want to try to save her,' Jenny recalled pleading with the vet. 'I know you have special liquid formula and vitamins.'

Determined to perform a miracle and save an angel, Jenny's girls volunteered for kitten-care duty. Every two hours one of them would feed Angel with an eye dropper filled with liquid food, medicine and love.

'Every afternoon, before my girls arrived home from school, I'd place Angel's lethargic little body on my lap and gently stroke her from head to tail,' explained Jenny. 'We'd watch my favourite afternoon television show together.'

Despite the vet's doubts, Angel soon put on weight and recovered to become the prettiest and most affectionate cat Jenny had ever owned.

For eight years, Angel pranced into Jenny's lounge room every afternoon to watch television with her. While Jenny sat on the couch, Angel would jump up and perch on the back rest just behind Jenny's head.

'Angel would gently paw at my left shoulder, as if massaging it. Then she'd move her head closer to the nape of my neck and gently purr into my left ear,' explained Jenny. 'Sometimes her whiskers tickled my neck and I'd laugh.'

Then six months ago, Angel didn't jump up on the back rest behind Jenny. Instead, she laid herself on Jenny's lap as if she were a sick kitten again.

'I stroked Angel's body like I used to all those years ago, and that is when I felt the lump,' said Jenny.

Jenny again rushed Angel to the vet. The news was devastating. Angel had a voracious form of bone cancer.

'I felt sick, Mitchell,' said Jenny. 'Angel had beaten the odds. How could this be happening to her after all her little body had gone through? It wasn't fair.'

'Her body is riddled with cancer,' Jenny recalled the vet saying. 'It would be cruel to make Angel suffer to her natural end.'

Jenny was faced with the most heartwrenching and difficult decision ever. She had to choose whether to end her little Angel's life.

After agreeing that a gentle death was the least Angel deserved and holding her until the end, Jenny cried for days. She couldn't eat and sleep evaded her. 'I felt so guilty,' said Jenny. 'I felt as if I had betrayed Angel, stolen her life, and robbed my girls of her love.' Jenny was inconsolable. Then, the day before her appointment to see me, her little Angel came to the rescue.

Jenny was sitting on the couch watching her favourite television show, when she felt a solid thump on the back rest behind her head.

'I was in disbelief, Mitchell. I felt a warm padding sensation on my left shoulder. A calming purr drifted into my left ear. As it did, all my feelings of sadness and guilt washed away. My heart filled with a sense of love, devotion and loyalty.'

'That was your little Angel visiting,' I said.

'What do you mean?' asked Jenny.

'She is trying to comfort you and let you know you did the best thing for her,' I said.

Jenny smiled.

'Angel wants you to forgive yourself and be happy again,' I continued.

For the first time in months, Jenny cried tears of joy.

Losing a pet who has been a valued member of a loving family isn't easy. For some people the grief experienced is just as heartbreaking and intense as losing a loved one. That's why it gives me so much joy to pass on messages from departed pets when they visit during readings.

If you've lost a pet, take comfort in the understanding they never pass alone. There's always a loved one in the Spirit World waiting to collect them. Sometimes it can even be another departed pet that guides them safely to the Afterlife.

Our departed pets can and do return to the physical world. Like Angel the cat, many return to give much-needed love and comfort. Others return because their arrival marks the delivery of an important message. But most of the time departed pets return simply to say *hello*.

Sensing Mitzi

My dear friend Susan had a beautiful part Persian calico cat called Mitzi. Besides her sweet nature, Mitzi had the knack of meowing what sounded exactly like 'he-llo'. As you can imagine, there were many stunned looks from those lucky enough to be greeted by Mitzi.

Sadly, Mitzi became quite ill and Susan rushed her to the vet. During the night, Susan heard Mitzi cry out to her.

'I awoke, sat upright and then questioned whether my feelings of dread about Mitzi were just an anxious dream,' said Susan.

Several hours later, while sitting with her father at the breakfast table, Susan shared her fears.

'Dad, I think Mitzi has passed away.'

Within the hour Susan's phone rang. Her heart sank as soon as she heard the vet's voice.

'Mitzi has passed, hasn't she?' asked Susan, before the vet got a chance to deliver the sad news.

The vet was surprised and asked Susan how she knew.

'I heard her cry out to me,' said Susan.

Remarkably, Mitzi was able to broadcast a final farewell to Susan the night she passed.

Some years later I was sitting with Susan in her home. I was drawn to particular spot near her sage-coloured curtains, just in front of the heater.

'Susan, the spirit of a small animal is sitting in front of the heater,' I said.

Susan smiled. 'That was Mitzi's favourite spot,' she said.

Just to show me, Susan swept the area with her EMF (electromagnetic field) meter. The lights instantly lit up – a strong reading indicating the presence of Mitzi – not that either of us needed any further proof.

Sensing when your departed pet is visiting doesn't require you to have any special equipment. Yolanda, a client of mine, leaves a basket of pet toys in her laundry despite it being two years since her adorable little Chihuahua, Dakota, passed. More than once, Yolanda has awoken to the sound of squeaking, only to find Dakota's toys scattered all over the laundry floor – just as she loved to leave them.

If you've lost a much-loved pet, remind yourself that departed pets will always be a special part of your family – no matter where you are. Mitzi the cat still visits Susan, even though Susan has moved house. When Mitzi returns to the physical world the characteristics of her visits are the same – quiet and demure. Dakota the Chihuahua, on the other hand, still scatters toys and ensures a give-away squeak marks his visit during the small hours of the morning. Even Angel the cat continues to create the sensation of her body landing on the back rest of Jenny's couch while she's watching 'their' favourite afternoon television show.

Returning pets are very clever when it comes to leaving calling cards. They'll use their personality and quirky character traits to let you know they are around. So talk to them during the day and keep their favourite toys on standby. In time, you'll learn to sense when your departed pets are visiting.

Just as we can sense the return of a departed pet, our pets can sense the return of a departed loved one. Dogs typically start barking for no apparent reason or race to a particular room as if called. One friend of mine says she knows exactly when her departed grandmother is visiting because her dog sits in front of her photograph and barks.

I've seen dogs raise one ear as their master

in Spirit speaks to them. Other clients have reported seeing their dogs tilt their heads to one side and wag their tails as if being patted by an invisible person.

Cats too can mark the arrival of a departed loved one. Some cats purr and stretch as if being stroked. Others meow and jump up onto empty chairs and settle themselves as if in the lap of a loving owner.

Penny's slippers

'After my father died I inherited his house and Penny, his Cavalier King Charles Spaniel,' explained Geraldine.

Before Geraldine's father, Lloyd, passed, he and Penny had a nightly routine. Lloyd would sit in his favourite armchair. At 7 p.m. on the dot Penny would run upstairs and fetch his slippers from the master bedroom. Then she would run back down the stairs, prance into the lounge room, and gently place the slippers on the carpet in front of Lloyd's feet.

After Lloyd had wriggled his feet into his slippers, he would take Penny into the kitchen and open a can of her favourite dog food. While Penny was eating her dinner, Lloyd would make a cup of tea and smoke his pipe. Then they'd both return to his chair. Penny would curl up in Lloyd's lap, watch television and eventually fall asleep.

'It broke my heart to see Penny set Dad's slippers down in front of his empty chair every night and patiently wait for him to show,' said Geraldine.

Try as she might, Geraldine could not break Penny out of her routine. Geraldine even tried hiding the slippers, but that only caused Penny more distress.

As the weeks passed Penny ate less until she refused to eat at all. Her tail drooped and her coat lost its healthy shine. Even her happy bark was silenced by her canine despair.

'One night I put Dad's slippers on and walked into the kitchen hoping Penny would follow me and eat something. But she didn't. Her eyes remained fixed on Dad's chair,' said Geraldine.

Realising Penny was fretting her life away, Geraldine stood in the kitchen one night, closed her eyes, opened her mind and said, 'Dad, if you can hear me, please visit. Penny needs you.'

Two days later, Geraldine was preparing her evening meal. The kitchen clock read two minutes to seven.

Out of the blue, Penny barked her happy bark. Not believing her own ears, Geraldine raced into the lounge room. She found Penny sitting in front of her dad's slippers, wagging her tail with excitement and looking up at his chair. Her head bobbed from side to side as if Geraldine's dad were lovingly ruffling her ears.

'Totally ignoring me, Penny trotted into the kitchen – as if Dad was right by her side,' said Geraldine. 'I was quick to put plenty of food in her bowl.'

Penny finished her dinner without any fuss and trotted back into the lounge room as if following Geraldine's dad.

'Much to my amazement, Penny yapped, jumped up onto Dad's chair and curled up as if she was on his lap,' said Geraldine. 'But the most astonishing thing of all was I could smell tobacco smoke – just as if Dad was smoking his pipe.'

Yet, when Geraldine looked, her father's pipe lay dormant and dusty in his ashtray, right where he had left it the night he passed.

How incredible! In a moment of great need, Geraldine's dad answered his daughter's prayer with what I am sure will be the first of many return visits.

While our pets react in very clear ways to communicate the arrival of a departed loved one, can their natural sensory perception extend beyond the ordinary to make extraordinary medical discoveries?

Not so long ago, Julie, a client of mine, told

me an intriguing story about her mother's cat, Ginger.

Ginger

'Mum and Ginger became a bit of a legend in our neighbourhood,' said Julie. 'So much so my kids used to take Grandma and Ginger to school for show and tell.'

Ginger was a huge tabby cat who, for the most part, acted like a dog. Yet his claim to fame was not his dog-like nature. Ginger was famous for another reason. He was the only cat known to 'take tea'.

'What that meant, Mitchell,' explained Julie, 'was that at three o'clock every afternoon Mum took freshly baked scones from the oven and made a fresh pot of tea. Ginger would jump up on their special afternoon tea table and sit opposite Mum – just like a best friend. While Ginger lapped at his tea, Mum would sip hers and feed him tiny pieces of freshly baked scone.'

Then one afternoon, it all changed. Ginger flatly refused to take tea. Instead, he sat on Julie's mum's lap. All Ginger was interested in doing was padding down her stomach – something he'd never done before.

'None of us could persuade Ginger to stop,' said Julie. 'And with a cat his size, you can't pick him up unless he wants you to.'

Julie's mum complained her stomach was sore, but Julie assumed it was because of Ginger. So she suggested Ginger be put out at night. At least that way her mum could get some respite from Ginger's constant attention.

'That was a mistake,' said Julie. 'Ginger meowed at the top of his lungs, climbed up every fly screen and scratched at every door and window until Mum let him in.'

Once back inside, Ginger ran straight to Julie's mum and started padding down her stomach again.

'Maybe we should take Ginger to the vet,'

Julie recalled suggesting to her mum. 'Perhaps he needs cat Valium.'

'I think it's me who needs to see the doctor,' Julie's mum responded. 'Lately I seem to have a lot of pain in my stomach.'

Julie scheduled a doctor's appointment the very next day. Two weeks later, Julie's mum was diagnosed with stomach cancer – and sadly, she passed six months later.

As in Ginger's case, the reactions of pets before the onset of illness are often misread or misunderstood. The meaning only becomes clear in hindsight.

Oscar

In 2005, Steer House nursing home in Providence, Rhode Island, adopted Oscar the cat. The staff felt pets made the place more like home. Creating a sense of home is important to them because Steer House is the last stop for people gravely ill with dementia. Patients admitted to Steer House are no longer able to speak or recognise their loved ones. Their days are spent lost in fragments of their failing memories.

One year after adopting Oscar the cat, nursing staff noticed that Oscar mostly kept to himself. His daily regime consisted – and still does – of marching from room to room sniffing and assessing patients. Rarely does he spend time with anyone – unless they only have hours to live.

Sensing death, Oscar snuggles alongside the dying patient, offering them peace and comfort. Remarkably, he stays by their side until their last breath has been taken. On past occasions, family members have requested that Oscar be removed from the room of their dying loved one. Like Ginger, Oscar became irritated to the point where he paced up and down the corridor until he was let back in.

So accurate are Oscar's incredible senses that nursing staff trust his intuition one hundred per cent. As soon as Oscar stretches out on the bed of a gravely ill patient, nursing staff immediately telephone the patient's family.

No one is quite sure how Oscar is able to predict impending death. However, I believe Oscar's psychic antenna senses when the physical body is about to expire and the soul is ready to leave.

I see Oscar as an earthly sentinel who offers great comfort to the dying. He stands guard ready to greet the departed loved ones who come to collect their friends and family members – offering a safe transition to the Afterlife.

Just as Oscar stands guard over the gravely ill, many dogs possess the miraculous gift of being able to accurately sense when their beloved owners are about to have epileptic seizures.

Brian, who is only twenty-three years old, told me he is new to epilepsy as a result of a serious head injury suffered during a workplace accident. Not so long ago, Brian discovered man's best friend was also man's best medicine.

Rex

'The first time I had a seizure after my accident, I was standing outside my local café talking to a friend when my dog, Rex, started acting strangely,' said Brian. 'First he just kept staring at me – as if I was doing something wrong.'

As anyone unaware would have done, Brian ignored Rex, but Rex was determined to be noticed. Even if that meant pushing at Brian's legs like a bulldozer.

'Rex was pushing me so hard I found myself forced away from tables and chairs into open spaces. It seemed safest, in case he actually managed to topple me,' explained Brian.

Moments later, Brian felt the onset of vagueness. His muscles started to tremor involuntarily. He collapsed on the ground just as violent spasms ricocheted through his entire body.

Brian's friend looked on in disbelief. Not only had Rex pushed Brian clear of tables and chairs but he used his body to cushion Brian's head throughout the fifteen-second seizure!

'Now every time Rex stares at me in that way, I know I'm about to have a seizure,' said Brian. 'Rex has given me a new lease on life.'

Brian now has the confidence to go out again. He even has a new job thanks to Rex's ability to accurately predict his seizures. And Rex isn't alone. There are many more accounts like Brian's throughout the world attesting to a dog's ability to predict the onset of a seizure. Some even stand guard over children.

Sampson

'My baby girl was born with severe epilepsy,' explained Gena. 'When Emma was just eighteen months old we were given Sampson, an Akita puppy. We really didn't want a dog because Emma needed so much care and supervision. Her fits were frequent and unpredictable.'

But as Gena and her husband soon discovered, Sampson was a blessing in a four-legged disguise.

'The first time I saw Sampson in action, I screamed,' said Gena. 'I honestly thought he was trying to attack Emma.'

However, Gena now understands that five minutes before Emma has a seizure, Sampson barks three times to sound the alarm. Then seconds before the oncoming seizure, Sampson forcibly sits Emma on the ground.

'Once Emma is on the ground, Sampson stands guard, protecting her convulsing body,' explained Gena.

While stories like these testify to the incredible predictive power of pets, some animals have proven themselves as great healers. It is well known that caring for a pet can lower blood pressure levels. Some pets even act as emotional barometers: they keep their owners calm in times of stress.

When an earthquake devastated the Japanese

city of Kobe in January 1995, thousands of people had to be housed in public buildings and gymnasiums. Despite the rules barring animals from public buildings, Japanese officials let people bring their pets. Why? Officials observed that the people who had their pets with them were calmer and coped better with the disaster.

Equally remarkable is the fact that many animals can sense an impending natural disaster and sound a warning long before sophisticated monitoring equipment. One example is the horrific underwater earthquake that shook the Indian Ocean floor on Boxing Day 2004. The resulting shock wave caused a massive tsunami which killed over 230,000 people in fourteen countries throughout Asia. Yet very few animals lost their lives.

Many hours before the earthquake, elephants were heard trumpeting wildly and seen racing toward higher ground, seabirds took to the air and would not land, chickens refused to lay eggs, cats became fearful and dogs refused to walk on their favourite beaches.

If it's possible for animals to predict earthquakes and tsunamis, what might an octopus be capable of? A famous oracle able to predict Word Cup soccer results – strange, but true.

Paul the psychic octopus

Paul the psychic octopus dazzled the world with his accurate World Cup predications. During his short lifespan he accurately predicted the winners of every German soccer match as well as the 2010 World Cup final in South Africa. Paul achieved this amazing feat by choosing to devour a mussel from one of two boxes placed in his tank, each bearing the flag of the competing teams.

If Paul had chosen the winning team once, the sceptical might have put it down to luck, but eight times in a row leaves no uncertainty about Paul's psychic ability.

Just as Paul could accurately pick the

winning teams, pets can pick winning personalities. Have you seen the way a dog will either run straight up to a person with their tail wagging, or stand back and rumble a low growl of caution?

I know a real-estate agent who takes her dog to meet people applying for rental properties. If he wags his tail, she knows they can be trusted to do the right thing by the property. If her dog growls, she knows to expect problems.

Another friend of mine said her dog always barked at her brother-in-law and would never let him pat her. Only years later, after her sister finally divorced, did she discover that her brother-in-law was extremely violent behind closed doors. Thankfully my friend's sister has since met a lovely gentleman – and my friend did take the precaution of introducing her dog to him! He passed with a wagging tail.

Cats too are good judges of character. One of my clients says her cat will arch its back, raise its fur and hiss at certain new acquaintances while politely welcoming others.

'Almost immediately I discover the people hissed at are of questionable character,' she said.

Another client has a white cocky. 'If he screeches when the door bell rings, I know it's a stranger at the door.'

Not only do animals use their psychic antenna to judge people and situations and avert danger, they can also become rescuers.

Max

Mabel, a seventy-year-old grandmother of three, told me of a terrifying time when she was looking after her three-year-old grandson, Jackson.

Mabel had taken her eyes off Jackson for no more than five minutes. In that time, he had vanished.

The feeling of impending danger struck Mabel's heart with a sickening blow. She hobbled as fast as she could to the front gate, ignoring the pain from her arthritic joints. Upon exiting the front door, her worst fears were realised – the front gate was open. When she reached the open gate, three-year-old Jackson was several hundred metres away, about to step down from the safety of the footpath onto a busy four-lane road.

Mabel could not run to her grandson in time and calling out would only increase the danger of him darting across the road in an effort not to be caught.

Panicked, Mabel recalled praying to herself, *Send me an angel.*

Like a bolt of lightning, Mabel's German Shepherd, Max, shot through the open gate and ran down the footpath toward Jackson. He was just a brown blur.

'It was unbelievable, Mitchell,' said Mabel. 'As Max approached he barked once. Jackson froze – just as if Max had shouted *stop*!'

Upon seeing Max, Jackson squealed with

delight and turned away from the dangerous road. He toddled toward Max with his arms open wide as if about to give him a big teddy-bear hug.

'Then, the oddest thing happened,' said Mabel. 'Max was on Jackson's right, shielding him from the road, but Jackson appeared to be holding hands with someone walking on his left side. No one was there.'

Then, just when Mabel thought the danger was over, a piercing screech followed by the crunch of colliding metal filled the air. To Mabel's horror, one car was spinning on the road while the other was skidding out of control toward the footpath, right where Jackson and Max were walking.

At that very moment Max forcibly nudged little Jackson's body out of harm's way. Seconds later the skidding car hit the German Shepherd with a sickening thud. Max yelped once then fell silent.

A quick-thinking pedestrian scooped

Jackson up in his arms and delivered him safely to Mabel. Other passers-by ran to the aid of the drivers.

There is no doubt pets can come to our rescue during the most incredible circumstances – just as Max did for little Jackson. I believe Spirit heard Mabel's pleas for help – proving not all angels have wings. Some have fur, four legs and a tail.

Animals truly are the most psychic beings on earth. Their lovable antics and quirky personalities go beyond bringing us joy and laughter. Their finely attuned psychic antenna can turn them into our loyal messengers, gallant saviours and heavenly healers.

CHAPTER 5

SENSING PSYCHIC

Have you ever been flashed a welcoming smile, only to feel that behind the mask of happiness hides a sad person? Perhaps you've sensed someone's eyes on you only to turn and find a stranger gazing your way. Or have other profound things happened to you? Has a spontaneous voice inside your mind given you timely advice or saved your life? Perhaps you've momentarily left your body, or seen curious colours spiralling around your loved ones. Every day, people from all walks of life sense the unspoken, read between the lines, find themselves magnetically drawn to another and experience events that defy logic.

Postcard from Miami

When Linda's hand reached inside her letter-box, she smiled. Finally, the postcard she'd been waiting for from Charlotte, her sister, had arrived.

'But Mitchell, something strange happened,' said Linda. 'As soon as I touched the postcard, I felt sick with worry.'

Confused by her feelings, Linda hugged Charlotte's postcard to her chest, hoping that her sense of worry would pass. 'I was so excited for Charlotte,' she told me. 'It made no sense to worry about her. She'd fallen in love with Steve and was finally flying to America to be with him.'

Charlotte had met Steve online in a chat room. While Linda initially had concerns about chat-room dating, Steve's heartwarming emails and obvious sincerity were enough to sweep any woman off her feet.

From the photographs Charlotte had seen, Steve was handsome. In his emails he wrote about his work as a surgeon in a busy Miami hospital. It was obvious hundreds of people trusted him with their lives. He was well off, drove a late-model silver Mercedes and had never been married. Plus he owned a picture-perfect home in Miami.

'How could Charlotte not fall head over heels in love with this man?' said Linda.

Despite all the evidence that Steve's love was sincere, Linda's sense of worry was so strong she felt compelled to book a reading with me.

'I just keep tracing my fingers over Charlotte's postcard, expecting to find a darker story hidden between the lines,' confessed Linda.

The instant I held Charlotte's postcard, I took a sharp breath. The card felt lopsided, like one end was heavier and more in love than the other. When I closed my eyes, the impression of a diamond engagement ring flashed through my mind and then transformed into a pair of handcuffs.

'This man Steve,' I said. 'He is not who he says he is.'

Linda's mouth dropped open in disbelief. 'Who is he, then?'

I ran my hand over Charlotte's handwriting once more and then flipped the postcard over to look at the picture on the front. A white yacht in full sail was heading into a glorious orange Key West sunset. Suddenly the chill of betrayal surged through my veins. I could feel Steve's intentions were cold, calculating and malicious.

'Steve is a cheat. He'll steal Charlotte's money,' I said.

Linda was horrified. 'What can I do to warn her?'

'Under *no* circumstances should Charlotte give this man any money,' I said.

After the reading, Linda told me later, she

stepped out of my office and immediately phoned Charlotte.

When Charlotte's mobile phone rang, she was standing in line at the bank – just minutes away from transferring one hundred thousand dollars into Steve's account. Noticing the call was from Linda she stepped out of the line to answer it, motioning the person behind her to step forward as the teller called 'next'.

It turns out that when Charlotte arrived in America, Steve could not wait to show her the floor plans of the new holiday home he was building in Key West. There was only one small problem. Steve was short of cash – one hundred thousand dollars short of cash. But given he'd already proposed, Charlotte saw no problem with investing her life savings to finish *their* magnificent holiday home. Thankfully, Linda's timely call put a stop to that, but only just.

How fortunate! Imagine what might have happened if Linda had ignored her spontaneous feelings when she first held the postcard? What if she had just stuck the postcard to her fridge and forgotten all about it? While Linda didn't save Charlotte from a broken heart, she certainly rescued her life savings.

Have you, like Linda, ever held an object and sensed energy coming from within it? Maybe instead of a postcard or letter you were holding a departed loved one's ring, watch or glasses. Perhaps you were looking at a photograph. The art of gaining impressions from objects is known as *psychometry*.

Psychometry

For some, psychometry comes naturally. For others it can be a spontaneous and unexpected experience. Either way, impressions can be received as images, sounds, smells, tastes, or emotions that relate to the past, present or future.

Newsflash

One morning, three years ago, Janet arrived at work to find a copy of the company's newsletter on her desk. Normally, Janet 'filed' newsletters in her wastepaper bin. But this morning was different. For some odd reason, Janet felt magnetically drawn to the newsletter.

Skipping the front page, Janet instinctively turned straight to page three. Staring at her was the smiling face of the new branch manager. Without rhyme or reason, Janet felt passionately connected to the man in the photograph. Even though she hadn't met him, excitement pulsed through her veins and she heard herself think, *I'll marry that man one day*. And she did – two years later.

For many, a picture paints a thousand words. When I hold a photograph the scene comes to life. I'm able to tune in and feel emotions. I can sense fears, see dreams and name desires. For me, the photo is no longer a moment frozen in time.

Little boy lost

Nothing is more traumatic than the thought of losing a child. Not so long ago I received a frantic call from Amanda, the mother of seven-year-old Zac. She'd given him permission to meet a friend in a nearby playground – so long as he returned home by lunchtime.

Lunchtime came and went. And by two o'clock Amanda was out of her mind with worry – especially when she arrived at the playground and saw there was no sign of her son or his friend.

Fearing the worst, Amanda had run home and telephoned the police. While understanding her concern, the police thought the most likely explanation was that Zac and his friend had gone off somewhere else to play and had lost track of time.

Amanda graciously accepted the fact she might have overreacted. However, when she started tidying Zac's toys away, a cold chill ran down her spine. Call it mother's intuition, Amanda just knew Zac was in serious trouble.

While I sat listening to Amanda over the phone, I sensed she was right. Fortunately, Amanda only lived around the corner from my office so I invited her to meet me there. I also instructed her to bring a recent photograph of Zac along with his favourite item of clothing.

When Amanda arrived at my office she handed me Zac's school football jumper. As soon as my fingers touched the wool blend fabric I felt the robust energy of an active little boy. The sort of boy who would climb the tallest tree only to turn around and shout, 'Help, I can't get down.'

'I feel cold and wet,' I said to Amanda, as goosebumps prickled my skin. 'I can hear running water and I'm trying to climb up something green but I keep slipping backward.'

When I tuned into Zac's photograph I felt the physical effort he was making to climb up, but it was followed by overwhelming frustration. I felt trapped.

'Zac is in some sort of drain,' I said.

Then Spirit created a picture in my mind's eye of a strong hand reaching down and clasping onto a smaller, softer hand.

'But don't worry,' I continued, 'a man will rescue Zac.'

Less than ten minutes later, Amanda's mobile phone rang. As I predicted, Zac had been found. He was alive and well, although cold and wet.

After playing in the park, Zac's friend went home and left Zac to continue his adventures on his own. The only trouble was he slipped and slid down a steep grass embankment into a storm-water drain. Try as he did, Zac couldn't climb out because the wet grass proved too slippery. Fortunately, only a slow flow of water was coursing through the drain that day. Had it been winter, the ending might not have been so happy.

In my experience, clothing and personal items can reveal much about their owners. But even more astonishing is jewellery. Rings, watches, pendants, charms and bracelets can have more than sentimental value. They can store cherished memories and closely guarded secrets – as Christina discovered.

Ring of truth

'When I was little,' explained Christina, 'I used to ask Dad if he was a secret agent.'

Christina felt her dad's job was to keep big secrets safe. That belief gave her great comfort because she always felt something stood between her and her father's deepest love. 'It was like Dad kept a part of his heart hidden from me,' she said.

As Christina matured into a woman, she let go of her childhood insecurities about her father. After all, time is a great healer. But on the day Christina's father died, a nurse handed her a plastic bag holding her father's signet ring.

Christina recalled finding a quiet place to sit. She took the signet ring out of the bag and slid it over her middle finger. Even then it wasn't a firm fit. But in that moment, Christina was instantly overwhelmed by an emotion she thought she'd laid to rest. 'Suddenly I felt like I was back in the past and that Dad was hiding a part of his heart from me again,' she said.

Slipping the ring off, Christina held it up to one eye – like a jeweller inspecting a diamond. That was the moment Christina discovered the name *David* engraved on the inside.

'In that instant, I just knew David was the thing Dad had been hiding from me.'

Christina spent the next five years trying to unlock the mystery of David. Who was he? And why was his name carved on the inside of her father's signet ring? Yet, despite her best detective efforts, every clue about David led her to a dead end. That's when she booked a reading with me.

'Are you sure you want to know the answers?' I asked, after Christina had handed me her father's signet ring. 'Some things are better left unsaid.'

'I need to know,' said Christina. 'Otherwise *I'll* never rest in peace.'

I closed my eyes and wrapped my fingers around the ring. Heat radiated from it as my mind filled with impressions, feelings, words and scenes that belonged to an earlier time – long before Christina's father was married.

'Now I have your dad in Spirit here with me – he's showing me you're one of two,' I said.

Christina stared at me, confused.

'Do you have a brother?' I asked.

'No,' she answered. 'I'm Dad's only child.'

As I continued with the reading more images came to me. I was shown a man in poor health sitting at his writing desk. I then sensed another man wearing a suit opposite him. I heard the word *Will.* And then I saw it – the answer Christina had been searching for.

'Your father left you a letter with his will,' I explained. 'But the envelope fell out of the file. I feel it's stuck or in a place it shouldn't be. With the letter is a photograph of a woman and a baby boy.'

Christina just stared at me – unable to fully grasp the meaning of what I was saying. 'But my dad was happily married to my mum for over thirty years. Are you saying there was another woman?'

Even I sat still for a moment, double-checking the images and impressions I was receiving. 'I definitely feel your father has a son he's kept a secret,' I said, gently.

Christina's eyes widened with disbelief.

'Your father says, *Find the missing envelope*,' I added.

Twelve months later I received a thank-you email from Christina. After her reading that day, she contacted her father's solicitor. Despite a thorough search of the solicitor's files, the envelope I described could not be found. It wasn't until some time later that it appeared.

One winter's afternoon, while sitting at her father's writing desk, Christina found herself lost in thought.

I don't know why, but I leant down and yanked open the bottom drawer with a little bit too much gusto, wrote Christina.

The drawer slid open with such force it dislodged from the runners. When Christina knelt down to right the drawer and reinsert it, she noticed a dusty white envelope lying flat in the space underneath where the bottom drawer slid in and out.

Christina retrieved the envelope, blew off the dust and opened it. Inside she found the letter and photograph I had seen in my visions. Christina shared part of that letter in her email:

Dear Christina,

... You will always be my number one daughter. But what I could never find the

courage to tell you was that you have a half-brother – his name is David. Just before your mother and I were engaged, I had an affair ... please find it in your heart to forgive me.

Remarkable! Who would have thought a signet ring could be the keeper of such a lifelong secret? While the truth was confronting for Christina, the ending was meant to be.

Thank you, Mitchell, wrote Christina. *Dad's letter and the photograph helped me find David. He's the spitting image of my dad. I now understand why Dad kept a special place in his heart for him. I would have too. He's the most amazing brother. I'm so happy I found him.*

If there is one thing helping thousands of people has taught me, it is that life never travels in a straight line. Our journey twists and turns and there is always something new to deal with, even for me.

One sunny summer afternoon my last client

for the day asked me the most unusual question. 'Is it possible for two chairs to be a couple?'

Until death do us part

Lunchtime, several months ago, Jacquie was scurrying past the window of her local second-hand furniture store when a voice inside her head said, *Look in here*. So she did. As soon as Jacquie stepped inside the store she saw exactly the antique wingback chair she had been searching for.

As she sat down in the chair and placed her arms on the comfy armrests, she gently pushed back to test the chair's rocking mechanism. The springs were worn but the chair itself didn't slump to one side or feel uneven.

'I was just thinking how perfect the chair was when I was overwhelmed with a sense of love,' explained Jacquie. 'It felt like the chair was hugging me.'

Yet, as soon as Jacquie flagged down the salesman and said, 'I want to buy this chair.

When can you deliver?' the sense of love dissolved into a great sadness. Confused, Jacquie turned to the salesman and remarked, 'How odd. Now I feel sad because I'm buying this chair.'

'That's because it is one of a pair,' Jackie recalled the salesman responding.

She eyed the salesman quizzically and then scanned the rest of the chairs surrounding her and said, 'Where? I don't see another one like it.'

The salesman smiled, turned and proceeded to pick his way through a field of chairs. Jacquie watched on with interest as the salesman stopped behind a well-worn antique leather smoking chair. He placed his hands on the back rest as if the chair itself were a dear friend and said, 'The chair you're sitting in and this one belonged to my parents.'

'So why are you selling them?' asked Jacquie.

Jacquie said the salesman hesitated and then

answered, 'My wife won't have them in the house. They're old and don't match.'

Jacquie stood up, walked over to the salesman and sat down in the leather smoking chair. 'Oh, this is delightful. This chair reminds me of my grandfather. I'll take them both.'

I sensed that Jacquie was intuitively reading the loving bond and special memories imprinted on the chairs. According to what the salesman told her, his parents had spent many years reading, laughing, talking and sipping red wine by an open fire in those chairs. It was almost as if Jacquie herself was sensing their original marriage vows – 'until death do us part'.

Just as Jacquie felt she was hugged by a chair, how often have you walked into a building and thought, *If only these walls could talk*? For those skilled at psychometry – the walls can and do talk. Like jewellery, clothing and personal items, buildings can store memories of past events. That's why when you tour historic buildings, old castles or intriguing ruins you can almost see the dramas that took place in certain rooms replaying themselves, or sense mystery stepping out from within the walls, and hear secrets being whispered out in the hallways.

A friend of mine recently visited the Grand Canyon – one of the world's seven natural wonders. Yet, despite the incredible landscape and panoramic vistas, she was overcome by a sense of heartbreak and loss. When she mentioned this to her Native American tour guide he said, 'My ancestors fought many battles on these lands. Few were won and many were lost.'

Incredibly, my friend was tuning in with her feet. She sensed the vibrations of victory along with all the tears that once spilled onto the Grand Canyon's hallowed grounds.

Auras

Much like light surrounds a candle flame or an

invisible cloud of perfume surrounds a flower, we each have an invisible field of energy. Known as the aura, this field is an extension of our body's unique vibrations.

Spiritual leaders like Mahatma Gandhi and the Dalai Lama have far-reaching auras that inspire greatness worldwide. Throughout his life Gandhi modelled non-violent practices and encouraged the people of India to find peace within. The Dalai Lama travels the world inspiring hundreds of individuals to find their true life path through meditation and self-reflection.

Many people sense the energies and auras of others without even realising it. Have you ever sat next to a stranger on a crowded bus, train or plane and instantly liked or disliked them? Perhaps you've glanced at your best friend and immediately sensed what was on her mind. Maybe you've stopped without hesitation to assist a stranger because you felt there was nothing to fear and much to be gained by helping.

Whenever we come into contact with another person we feel their energy; we sense their aura. Children are naturals when it comes to detecting the energy around them. Without training or practice, children tune in as easily as we turn on the television. They see the people around them in their true colours.

Cupcakes

Recently, I had a grandmother arrive for her reading. Accompanying her was her five-year-old granddaughter.

'Hello, Mitchell,' said the little girl. 'You'll never guess what colour granny's light is today.'

'Red,' I said, looking at her grandmother's red dress.

'No, silly,' said the little girl. 'Can't you see?'

'See what?' I asked, realising the little girl was referring to her grandmother's aura.

'Granny's light is *blue* today.'

'Really,' I said. 'What made her light blue?'

The little girl hesitated and pulled at the hem of her skirt before answering, 'Granny's light is always blue when she misses Poppy.'

This sweet little grandchild was intuitively sensing her grandmother's private moments of sadness simply because she tuned in and observed colour changes in her aura. But I have to say the most priceless moment came just as the two were leaving. The little girl beckoned me closer and then whispered in my ear, 'Granny's light is pink when she bakes me cupcakes.'

Family portrait

It wasn't until near the end of Owen's reading that I remembered to ask, 'Do you have any photographs you'd like to show me before we finish?'

To my surprise, Owen handed me a scroll of white paper.

'Bailey, my six-year-old son, drew this,' said Owen.

As I opened the roll of white art paper, a family of stick figures greeted me: Mum, Dad, three children and a blob with eyes and a smiley mouth – presumably the baby. Typically, Dad was wearing rectangular trousers and a square shirt with sleeves. Bailey's brothers were clothed similarly to Dad, but with rectangular shorts instead. Mum was wearing a triangular skirt offset with pointy triangular shoes. But what leapt up from the page was that each family member was encased in a beautiful rainbow-coloured aura – all except Bailey's mum. While everyone else was encased in a bubble of vibrant yellow, sunset orange, forest green and tranquil blue, his mum was being consumed by swirls of grey and black.

'Is my wife going to die?' asked Owen.

It was easy to see why Owen feared such an outcome. Even I had to admit, there was something unsettling about the way Bailey had depicted such a dark aura around his mum – but it certainly wasn't death.

Several seconds after I viewed the drawing, a woman from the Spirit World stepped forward.

'I sense your wife's mother is here with us – did she pass recently?' I asked.

'Yes,' answered Owen.

'She is telling me your wife needs help,' I continued. 'The dark clouds Bailey has drawn represent all the grief she's holding back.'

Like many dedicated, loyal and selfless women, Owen's wife was trying to cope with losing her beloved mother in silence. But as Bailey so innocently had drawn – grief was silently consuming his mother. Thankfully, Owen was a caring, loving and responsible husband.

'Thank you, Mitchell,' he said. 'For the first time I feel like I know what to do to repay my wife for all the support and love she's given to us over the years.'

Perhaps Bailey's innocent portrayal of his

family's auras explains why so many cave paintings and religious figures were drawn with halos and lines radiating around the outside of their bodies.

Auras, just like rainbows, can contain many colours. But unlike a rainbow, the colours change and layer themselves from moment to moment depending on moods and emotions. I just love it when happy couples walk into my office and spirals of soft pink swirl around in their auras. The same goes for those who meditate or practise yoga regularly. Healing greens and peaceful blues dominate as their personal energy radiates peace, harmony and wellbeing.

In a similar way, colour in clothing also reflects meaning. Certain Buddhist monks wear orange robes because the brightness of orange repels darkness and ignorance. Purple, in medieval times, denoted nobility or royalty. Native American culture has long held the belief that blue, white and yellow are sacred healing colours.

While the colours inside an aura constantly swirl, intermingle and change depending on the person's thoughts, feelings and wellbeing, one or two colours tend to dominate at any given time.

Can you recall the little girl who whispered in my ear, 'Granny's light turns pink when she bakes me cupcakes.' Pink is the colour of passion, unconditional love, sensitivity, softness and compassion. And what grandmother wouldn't radiate pink light when baking for such an adorable little granddaughter?

A particularly gifted student at one of my psychic development workshops once asked, 'Why is your aura green here but gold at your seminars?'

I explained green is the colour of healing, teaching, balance and self-love. I like to project green light when I teach because I sense it helps my students to learn. Whereas gold is the colour of spirituality, prayer and protection – exactly the energies I need when communicating with the Spirit World.

Snap shot

A couple of years ago I was involved in a photo shoot for *That's Life* magazine. The photographer was highly skilled and prided himself as one of the best in the business. But to his absolute dismay, every shot he took of me that day was ruined by an unusual pink light around my head. The photographer was beside himself. He double-checked his camera and printing equipment. No technical faults could be found anywhere – not even with the studio lighting. In all his years of professional experience, nothing like that had ever happened to him. I tried to tell him not to worry: it was just my aura. I don't think he believed me, though.

The editor of *That's Life* magazine, on the other hand, was so amazed she decided to run the photographs with a sidebar story titled *Aura or Error?* Maybe you read it.

Today, special biofeedback photographic technology is giving everyone a chance to see incredible *simulations* of their own aura. Have you had photographs taken by such a camera? If you have two or more aura photographs, try comparing them. Are the colours completely different? Can you recall how you were feeling on each occasion? Or maybe, like me, you've had ordinary photographs developed with unusual halos of light around all or part of your body.

Just recently I was shown an intriguing photograph of a Siamese cat with the most hauntingly beautiful blue eyes. Around the cat's body were rays of amethyst and violet. I immediately sensed this cat was highly in tune with her owner and the Spirit World. Like people, pets too have auras.

Pet auras

Just as we can see energy changes in the auras of those around us, so do pets. That is why pets often give affection when we're feeling sad, or sit by our side when we need comforting, or bark to welcome us home. Some pets go as far as to stand guard when we feel threatened or let us know when they don't like a certain person.

Not so long ago I met Penny – a pet groomer and pet aura reader. She told me about one of her 'doggy' clients, Miss M.

Miss M was a normally sweet Maltese Terrier; she was usually easy to handle. But on this day Miss M was extremely temperamental and difficult. She wouldn't stay still; and she actually tried to bite Penny several times during the grooming session.

When Penny tuned into Miss M's energy, she noticed that Miss M's aura was entirely *beige* – which, according to Penny, reflects a change in the pet's environment. Penny also sensed Miss M wanted to get home fast and chase something or someone away. So when Miss M's owner came to collect her, Penny asked if Miss M had been her usual self. Miss M's owner chuckled. 'Miss M is always on her worst behaviour whenever my brother-in-law visits.'

Every living thing has an aura. Perhaps that explains why people who live hectic and stressful lives find patting their pet extremely relaxing – especially if their pet's aura is of a calming or healing nature. And maybe that's why so many of us flock to tranquil tropical islands, with their *white* beaches, *golden* sunsets, calm *blue* waters and peaceful *green* forests. Nature's colour and beauty radiates its own aura – one that refreshes our spirit, recharges our energy and replenishes our soul.

Soulmates

Have you ever met someone and instantly

'clicked' with them? Did your heart skip a beat? And within minutes, did you feel like you'd known each other a lifetime?

Every day I hear of the miraculous ways in which a wrong turn, missed appointment, or chance phone call leads to a meant-to-be meeting.

Compelling feelings

At the tender age of seventeen, Veronica arrived at her friend's party. She was so excited to be there, yet, only two hours later, that had all changed. Without any obvious reason, Veronica felt compelled to leave. The feeling was so strong, not even Veronica's girlfriend could persuade her to stay and enjoy the fun.

With less than one kilometre to travel before reaching home, Veronica noticed a pleasantly dressed guy in his mid-twenties hitch-hiking near a bus stop.

Although hitch-hiking in the early 1970s was common, it was way out of character for

Veronica to consider giving *any* stranger a lift. Yet, the 'compelling feeling' that urged her to leave the party was now making her stop and ask the hitch-hiker if he wanted a lift.

When Veronica's car slowed to a stop, the hitch-hiker leant down to look at her through the open driver's window.

'Where are you headed?' asked Veronica.

The hitch-hiker smiled before answering. And in that instant, Veronica felt her heart skip a beat as she sensed a familiarity that defied all logic. Fortunately, the hitch-hiker lived in the suburb just before Veronica's – so she said 'hop in'.

In the car, conversation flowed easily. Within the space of two minutes the guy was no longer just a hitch-hiker. He was Jeremy. Within ten minutes, Veronica felt like she'd found a long-lost friend. Veronica didn't realise Jeremy was feeling just as inexplicably connected to her until she stopped outside his home. Like Veronica, Jeremy didn't want the night to end.

So he asked Veronica if she'd like to get something to eat. She didn't hesitate.

By the time Veronica and Jeremy had finished their meal they knew a huge amount about each other's lives, dreams and ambitions. Veronica was convinced they were a match made in heaven. She gave Jeremy her number and he promised with all his heart to call but, for whatever reason, he never did.

Five years elapsed. During that time Veronica met someone else and was engaged to be married. The weekend before her wedding Veronica was out shopping at a major department store. As she was standing on the escalator heading down to the next floor, she was suddenly compelled to look to her left. Almost opposite her on the escalator heading up was Jeremy – the hitch-hiker from five years earlier. As Veronica's eye caught Jeremy's, her heart skipped an unmistakable beat. He too visibly hesitated. But Veronica kept her feelings in check. After all, she was getting married in less than a week.

Thirteen years later Veronica's life had changed direction once again. She was divorced and living on her own – she hadn't had children with her husband. While carrying out small renovations to her home, Veronica placed an advertisement in the local newspaper. She was hoping to sell her smaller rainwater tank. Veronica was bitterly disappointed when, out of all the people in Brisbane, only one person responded to her advertisement. Fortunately, the man was eager to see her tank and arranged to visit that afternoon.

As a strange car rolled to a stop in Veronica's driveway, a feeling of familiarity washed over her. As the man who'd been driving stepped out of the car and started walking toward her, the sense of familiarity intensified. Veronica could not quite put her finger on why, but as soon as the man stood in front of her and introduced himself, she realised why he felt familiar and her heart skipped another beat. Standing in front of Veronica was Jeremy – the hitch-hiker she'd picked up from the bus stop when she was just seventeen.

Within minutes of talking to each other, it was like the dinner they shared eighteen years ago was only yesterday. Veronica and Jeremy started dating almost immediately, married shortly after, and started a family. Today Veronica and Jeremy are enjoying their prime and are still very much in love.

The universe works in the most mysterious ways. Veronica's willingness to trust her 'compelling feelings' allowed divine timing to reunite her with Jeremy – her 'soulmate' as some might say. But I sense we can have more than one soulmate. So I prefer to call soulmates – *soul connections*.

Affairs of the heart

Twelve months ago, Jacinta sat in front of me feeling very confused. Even though she loved her husband dearly and truly felt that he was her soulmate, she found herself inexplicably 'falling' for her new business partner.

'The connection I feel with my business partner is just as strong as the feelings I have for my husband,' confessed Jacinta.

When I tuned into the situation I sensed Jacinta and her business partner were indeed deeply connected, but they were *not* destined to become lovers, as Jacinta feared.

'What you're feeling is a soul connection, but it's not a romantic one,' I explained. 'Your business partner has entered your life as a guide and mentor, not as a lover.'

Jacinta left my office that day excited about her new understanding of soul connections and the bright future that lay ahead for her business.

As in Jacinta's case, not all soul connections are destined to become romantic partners, lovers or spouses. Throughout life's journey soul connections can arrive in the form of friends, mentors, family members, business partners and even pets. The curious thing about soul connections is that they don't always necessarily mirror our personality, likes, dislikes or philosophies and beliefs.

Some soul connections are destined to *gift* us with challenges – and they usually don't move on from our lives until the teachings and wisdoms they bring are understood. However, there are many other instances where we'll connect with someone so extraordinary we're convinced they're an 'angel on earth'. For whatever reason, divine timing has placed this person in our lives just as we're about to begin a new project we need help with, prepare for a major change or navigate the lessons we've agreed to learn during this lifetime. In some instances these cherished and deep soul connections are brief – yet they always leave behind a valuable, lifelong legacy.

The gift

A friend of mine had a little girl who was loving school up until grade three. Then, for some inexplicable reason, she started to struggle with her schoolwork and found it difficult to participate successfully in class activities. Her regular teacher put it down to her being a strong-willed child who wanted to do things her own way. Then, halfway through the year, the regular teacher left on maternity leave. The moment the relief teacher set eyes on my friend's little girl, something special resonated deep within them both. An instant and very special bond formed between the pair.

'They just "clicked",' said my friend. 'It's like they were sisters in a past life.'

Two weeks later, my friend received a phone call from the relief teacher asking if they could meet. During their parent–teacher chat the relief teacher asked my friend, 'How long has your little girl had her hearing problem?'

Naturally, my friend was devastated. Not

once had she even suspected her daughter had a hearing problem.

'Your daughter is so bright,' said the relief teacher, 'she's been able to mask her hearing difficulties by lip-reading.'

For the next six months, the relief teacher took my friend's daughter under her wing. She placed her at the front of the class and even visited her at home. Despite the age gap, they were like sisters and best friends all rolled into one. When it came to my friend's little girl wearing her new hearing aids to school, the relief teacher made sure none of the children teased her. Yet, despite the miraculous connection the two shared, their friendship ended. The relief teacher was offered a permanent teaching position at another school hundreds of kilometres away.

As hard as it was for my friend's daughter to say goodbye to her cherished friend, the relief teacher left her with a valuable, lifelong legacy

– never let anyone or anything hold you back in life.

Twin connections

Twins also share an intriguing psychic connection. Every day the friends, family and spouses of twins bear witness to this incredible bond.

'I'm married to a twin,' said Martha, one of my clients. 'Every time my husband gets grumpy for no reason, I tell him to call his brother.'

After years of marriage Martha has learnt to sense when her husband is unconsciously tuning into his twin brother's moods.

Cynthia, another client of mine, is also a twin. 'When my sister went into labour with her first baby, I felt her contractions,' said Cynthia. 'Another time, she had a horrific migraine and *I* was the one who vomited.'

Like Cynthia, reports worldwide show how twins can and do sense symptoms or thoughts belonging to each other – even when the other twin is in the Spirit World.

Words of warning

When I met Max, a 24-year-old blond surfer, I immediately sensed he was a twin. Underneath his sun-bleached dreadlocks and laidback personality, I also felt a deep sadness.

Two years earlier, Max had lost his twin brother, Ryan, in a tragic surfing accident. Ryan was knocked unconscious by a surfboard and drowned before Max could save him.

'The thing is, I can still hear Ryan's voice in my head,' said Max.

Initially Max put hearing Ryan's voice down to grief, but when it continued Max began to think otherwise. That's why he came to see me.

'I think my brother's voice is guiding me,' confessed Max. 'Is that nuts or what?'

When I asked Max why he thought his brother's spirit might be guiding him he answered, 'Because he saved my life.'

Max was holidaying at Gracetown near Margaret River, one of Western Australia's top surfing spots. He'd planned to surf Cowaramup Bay on the morning of 17 August 2010.

'I woke early,' said Max. 'I was strapping my board onto the roof-rack of my rented four-wheel drive when I heard Ryan's voice inside my head say, *Don't surf today.*'

Max shrugged off the words of warning and drove to Cowaramup Bay as planned. But when he arrived, something even stranger happened.

'As I stood in the carpark looking down at the lines of surf rolling into shore, I felt a dark shadow pass over me,' explained Max. 'The feeling was so eerie, it spooked me.'

Unable to shake the eerie feeling, Max abandoned the idea of an early morning surf and instead decided to drive over to Margaret River for breakfast.

'At the time I can remember thinking, *I never put breakfast before an early morning surf – what is wrong with me?*'

While driving back to Cowaramup Bay several hours later, Max had the sudden urge to listen to the local radio station. Leading the news was a breaking story about a man who had been attacked earlier that morning by a great white shark while surfing alone at Cowaramup Bay.

'I felt sick to my core,' said Max. 'That could have been me.'

Initially Max was confused by his 'inner voice' but I did my best to explain he was simply tuning into a natural psychic connection.

'Just as Ryan was connected with you in life, so he is in Spirit,' I said. 'Ryan will always hear your thoughts, just as you will hear his.'

The other me

Emily was three months old when Maxine adopted her from a Korean orphanage. From the day Emily first learnt to speak she was obsessed with an 'imaginary' sister whom she called *the other me*. That's why, at the tender age of five, Emily was sitting in front of me with her mum.

'Tell Mitchell what you want most in the whole wide world,' prompted Maxine.

'The other me,' replied Emily.

'Do you have a sister?' I asked.

'Yes,' replied Emily.

'No,' said Maxine. 'Only an older brother.'

'But there *is* another me, Mummy,' insisted Emily.

Maxine's despair surfaced in a flood of tears.

'I can't convince Emily otherwise,' sobbed Maxine. 'She cries at night for her sister. She draws pictures of her sister. She won't drink milk because it makes her sister's stomach hurt. She'll only wear blue because it's her sister's favourite colour.'

At that moment, a young woman stepped forward from the Spirit World.

'A kind young woman is here with us. Her love for Emily is very strong,' I said. 'But she is holding up one finger on both hands and bringing them together as I'm hearing the words *one of two*.'

Maxine looked at me blankly.

'Is it possible Emily is a twin?' I asked.

'Yes, Mummy,' chirped Emily. 'The other me.'

Nearly one year later, Maxine caught up with me after one of my seminars. It turns out she'd been reading a blog written by a woman who had adopted a Korean baby girl named Emma.

Emma was the same age as Emily. She too insisted there was 'another me'. She too wore only blue. She too drew pictures of an 'imaginary' sister and cried at night because she missed her. But what really stopped Maxine's heart midbeat was reading: *Emma is allergic to milk*. Maxine's Emily refused to drink milk because it hurt her 'imaginary' sister's tummy.

Maxine contacted the other mum and asked if they could exchange emails. When Maxine opened an attachment containing a photograph of Emma, she cried. Maxine might as well have been looking at a photograph of her very own daughter, Emily.

Many months later, the Korean orphanage confirmed Emily did have a sister. Maxine also discovered that Emma and Emily's maternal mother had died during childbirth. Sadly the mother's parents were too poor to raise two grandchildren. Giving one child to the orphanage was the only way of ensuring her survival. But as the months passed, it became clear they could not even afford to feed and clothe the remaining granddaughter. She too was handed over to the orphanage.

Unfortunately, no one at the orphanage realised the two girls were from the same family because they were handed over months apart. As a result, the girls were added to the records as individuals and adopted out accordingly. Miraculously, Emily and Emma were both adopted by Australian parents. What is even more incredible is that when DNA testing was finally carried out, it was proven that Emily and Emma were not only sisters, they were identical twins.

Out-of-body experiences

Have you ever drifted off to sleep, only to wake with a sudden jolt? What about flying in your dreams? Perhaps you've left your body during a period of great stress. It is out-of-body experiences like these that open a window to another world, giving everyday people extraordinary encounters.

Scent of Paris

When Fiona walked into my office, I could tell something was playing on her mind.

'Three weeks ago I went to bed early,' explained Fiona. 'The last thing I remember thinking was I wish I knew if Drake was going to marry me.'

Moments, minutes or hours later – Fiona wasn't sure which – she awoke to find herself in two places.

'It was the strangest thing,' she said. 'I could see my body asleep in my bed in Sydney but I was also standing in Drake's hotel room in Paris.'

Fiona felt like a ghost watching Drake prepare for bed. As her presence hovered in his hotel room the time display on the bedside clock caught her attention – *10.30 p.m., 5 July 2009*.

'As the time and date burnt themselves onto my memory, Drake stopped and gently sniffed the air,' said Fiona. 'I instantly felt guilty. I remembered I'd worn to bed the expensive French perfume he told me not to open.'

For one brief moment Fiona really thought Drake could smell her perfume, but in the next instant he shrugged his shoulders and turned away from where Fiona's out-of-body presence was hovering.

'Drake then slid his hand under his pillow and withdrew a photograph,' said Fiona. 'I knew it was a picture of me because I felt his soft, warm lips kiss mine as he kissed the photograph.'

But in that instant, a whooshing sound filled Fiona's ears. She felt herself being rapidly drawn back toward her body. Seconds later she was awake, sitting upright in bed – just as if she'd dropped straight down from the ceiling.

From that night on, Fiona had no doubt Drake would marry her. Even so, the strange experience weighed heavily on her mind. So she decided to test Drake when he returned home from Paris.

'I think it's cute how you keep a photo of me under your pillow,' teased Fiona.

'How on earth do you know that?' said Drake, totally surprised.

'I think I visited you in a dream or something,' said Fiona.

Drake raised one eyebrow, but it wasn't to ridicule Fiona.

'Ten-thirty Tuesday night, July fifth – did you open the perfume I told you not to?'

'Yes …' answered Fiona slowly.

It was at that point Fiona realised her out-of-body experience was real.

As Fiona's story demonstrates, if a heartfelt desire is strong enough it can create experiences that defy all logic.

Doug, another client of mine, found himself out of his body for a completely different reason.

Open heart

It wasn't even Doug's recent brush with death that brought him to see me. Nor was he interested in knowing whether he'd have another heart attack. Doug was sitting in front of me because a strange experience he had had was playing heavily on his mind.

'I still can't believe it,' said Doug. 'I woke up in the middle of open-heart surgery.'

My eyes widened. I couldn't think of anything more horrifying.

'But that's just it, Mitchell,' said Doug. 'I didn't wake up from the anaesthetic as such – I simply left my body.'

I was intrigued.

'I just hovered above the operating table, fascinated by the fact I couldn't feel any pain,' said Doug.

'How long were you out of your body?' I asked.

'I don't know, but it was long enough to hear the surgeon say to his assistant, "We're going to have monitor this patient closely for graft failure," and for a nurse to ask, "Is the increased risk due to his diabetes?" '

When Doug regained consciousness and was well enough to chat with the surgeon he asked, 'Is there a chance my bypass graft will fail like you said?'

Dough laughed when he recalled the dumbfounded look on the surgeon's face.

'He looked like a kid who'd been caught out by the truth,' chuckled Doug. 'And when I asked him whether the nurse was correct – was my bypass graft at risk because of my diabetes? – I could have knocked him over with a feather.'

'Who told you all that?' Doug recalled the surgeon asking.

'You did,' replied Doug. 'I woke up during the operation and heard you talking.'

I reassured Doug his out-of-body experience was nothing to worry about.

'Believe it or not,' I said, 'the phenomenon isn't as rare as you think.'

Recently, many prominent medical doctors have published books about out-of-body experiences. They're fascinating reading.

Just as out-of-body experiences can give astonishing answers and reveal much needed information, near-death experiences can change lives.

Not your time

One cold and rainy winter's night eighteen-year-old Levi sat behind the driver's wheel racing toward home. But as he manoeuvred into the last sharp bend before the straight stretch home, he realised too late that he was travelling too fast.

'I felt the car aquaplane and then enter an uncontrolled slide,' said Levi. 'There was nothing I could do except pray that I didn't hit a tree. But I wasn't so lucky.'

The next thing Levi remembered was standing on the dark roadside looking at the crumpled wreck of his car wrapped around a huge tree.

'The rain was hammering down hard, but I wasn't getting wet,' said Levi. 'Yet what confused me most was how my body could be slumped over the steering wheel while I was standing outside looking at it.'

Levi wasn't sure how long he stood staring at the wreck, watching steam hissing from the radiator and petrol escaping from the split fuel tank.

'When I finally understood I had died,' said Levi, 'I didn't panic. Peace and serenity surrounded me in the darkness.'

Then out of the darkness came a light much brighter than the sun.

'The odd thing was the light didn't hurt my eyes,' said Levi. 'It was filled with so much warmth and love I just started walking toward it.'

At that moment Levi's departed father appeared within the light.

'I felt Dad hug me, although his arms didn't move,' explained Levi. 'He told me it wasn't my time and that I should go back, but I didn't want to. I begged him to stay with me and talk. I missed him so much.'

Levi doesn't know how much time he spent with his departed father as time itself was irrelevant. Nor did he remember returning to his body. All he knows is that he woke up in a hospital bed five days after the accident.

Levi's injuries were extensive and his recovery was slow. While watching me on *The Morning Show* one day, Levi turned to his mother and asked if she could get him an appointment with me. When Levi's mother asked why, Levi replied he wanted to ask a question to which only I would know the answer.

That question was, 'Is it possible for me to see Dad again without dying?' I smiled when he asked me and introduced Levi to the idea of using his psychic antenna.

CHAPTER 6

PSYCHIC ANTENNA

Everyone is naturally psychic, but some people are more in tune with psychic signals than others. For instance, do you solve problems in your dreams, experience 'ah-ha' moments in the shower, or seem to *just know* something without knowing why you know it? Or maybe you get butterflies in your stomach when danger is near. Perhaps there has even been a time when you've glimpsed the future, heard voices from beyond, received profound messages in your dreams, or acted upon an impulse that has saved your life.

Sea angel

Two years ago, Jessica, thirty-five, survived a horrific explosion that killed her husband. But seconds before the faulty gas cylinder in the yacht they'd hired exploded, Jessica was saved by a fleeting glimpse of something that compelled her to investigate it further.

Nearing midday, Jessica's husband decided to drop anchor in a calm blue bay glistening with summertime brilliance. He wanted their tenth wedding anniversary to be picturesque and romantic.

Below deck, Jessica had just finished preparing a scrumptious grilled fish and fresh mango salad for lunch. But just as Jessica placed the beautifully presented meals on the small galley table, she thought she caught a glimpse of something white flash past the port-side window.

'Whatever I saw out the corner of my eye was immediately followed by an intense flapping sound,' explained Jessica. 'My husband didn't seem to notice so I instructed him to pour the wine and said, "I'll be back in a flash." '

Without further explanation, Jessica quickly climbed the ladder leading to the deck.

'Mitchell, I stood on deck and not a breath of wind stirred. Even the sails were oddly silent,' she told me.

But just as Jessica shrugged her shoulders and thought, *I must have imagined it*, the mainsail boom suddenly swung across and knocked her overboard. In the split second that it took for Jessica's body to hit the water and disappear below the surface, the yacht exploded.

'The muffled sound of that explosion still haunts me today,' said Jessica.

When Jessica surfaced she looked on in horror as huge orange flames rapidly engulfed the yacht.

'I couldn't get back to the boat to see if my husband was all right,' explained Jessica, as tears streamed down her cheeks. 'The burning heat was so intense I actually had to swim further away.'

Jessica screamed out her husband's name, but only the roaring flames answered her.

'At that moment I just knew I'd lost him,' cried Jessica.

People from all walks of life like Jessica intuitively receive snippets of psychic information that help them to avert danger, solve problems or predict the outcome of future events. As incredible as it may sound we can all receive psychic signals because we all have a psychic antenna.

Your psychic antenna receives *four* types of psychic signals. They are psychic *feeling*, psychic *hearing*, psychic *seeing* and psychic *dreaming*. But not everyone's psychic antenna will tune into all four psychic signals at once. Jessica, for example, investigated 'a fleeting glimpse' (psychic seeing) and an 'odd noise' (psychic hearing).

Like Jessica, many people find their psychic

antenna only tunes into one or two psychic signals at a time. Yet over time, they notice their antenna receives some signals better than others.

Psychic feeling

When you meet someone for the first time, can you instantly feel whether they are a 'good' or 'bad' person? Maybe your body responds in some way. I know my hands warm up or tingle when I encounter a certain type of person. For some, shaking hands is like looking directly into someone's heart. They can instantly feel the person's true emotions – and intentions. Maybe you don't even need physical contact. Perhaps you know when to be on guard or when to relax simply by feeling the energy that surrounds you.

People who tune into psychic feeling signals often start their sentences with 'I feel …' For example, 'I feel I can trust that person' or 'I feel my boss is a fun person, but puts on a stern face at work'. For these people, their psychic antenna is able to receive the psychic signals being broadcast by the people, places or objects around them. Sometimes psychic feeling people are not even aware they're receiving signals until a sudden and often uncharacteristic physical or emotional feeling catches them by surprise.

Sugar kisses

Shimmering under a sugar-crystal crust was a taste sensation Melissa had not expected. 'When I bit into what I thought was an ordinary doughnut my taste buds were instantly delighted,' she explained. 'Hidden inside was a ring of soft, sweet, cinnamon-infused apple.'

But when Melissa took her second bite she felt like the children's fairy-tale character Snow White. 'Sweetness swept through my body. I felt like I'd woken up from a deep sleep just in time to be kissed by a charming prince.'

The only problem was that Melissa's *prince*

was her charming local baker and all she had done was bite into a fresh apple and cinnamon doughnut in a bakery full of people.

'He sells dozens of doughnuts every day,' lamented Melissa. 'Surely I'm not the only woman who feels his sweet sugar kisses are hidden inside the doughnuts?'

Despite Melissa's light-hearted approach to a sweet problem, she was convinced her taste buds were telling her that her charming local baker was secretly harbouring romantic feelings for her.

'If I don't work out what on earth is making me feel this way, Mitchell,' said Melissa, 'I'll end up as round as a doughnut. I visit his bakery nearly every day! I can't help myself.'

Melissa and I laughed. But what she was experiencing was psychic feeling signals manifesting themselves through taste.

'You can taste whether food has been prepared with love, tension, sadness or happiness,' I explained.

And as the reading progressed, Spirit confirmed Melissa's taste buds were right. *Romance* was definitely in the air. Melissa's charming baker wasn't secretly infusing his doughnuts with a magic love potion. Instead, his sweet sugar-crusted doughnuts – with their soft cinnamon apple centres – were baked with love especially for Melissa.

What an ingenious way for the baker to display his affections without saying so in a shop full of customers.

'Trust your feelings and talk to your charming baker some more,' I said. 'His hidden sugar kisses are genuine.'

Butterfly feelings

'When I was five,' said fifty-year-old Debbie, 'my grandmother told me butterflies bring messages from the angels.'

So, as any inquisitive five-year-old would do, Debbie captured several butterflies and put them in glass jars.

'But I quickly learnt that butterflies couldn't even talk let alone deliver messages from angels,' said Debbie. 'So I dismissed my grandmother's words as *just* stories.'

Three years later, Debbie changed her mind.

'When I was eight years old I was sitting in class. Without cause or warning, I felt like I'd just dropped ten floors in an elevator,' explained Debbie. 'I raised my hand and was about to tell the teacher I didn't feel well when a bright orange butterfly flew in through the open window and landed on my desk.'

Debbie instantly knew that the butterfly had brought terrible news from home. That was confirmed two minutes later when the principal interrupted her class and asked Debbie to follow him outside.

'To this day I can still hear the principal telling me my house had burnt down and that my mother and grandmother had been rushed to hospital,' explained Debbie.

Another time, Debbie was in her early

thirties. She recalled waking up with the nagging feeling that she *must* see a doctor. 'It was crazy. I was very fit, ate a healthy diet, and looked fantastic. There was absolutely nothing wrong with me – so I ignored the feeling.'

Later that morning, Debbie was standing in line at her local dry-cleaning store waiting to be served. From out of nowhere, a bright orange butterfly landed on the woman standing in front of her.

'With each beat of its wings, the urge to see a doctor intensified,' said Debbie. 'I felt that if I didn't act, something terrible would happen to me – like the day our house burnt down.'

So Debbie phoned her doctor's surgery and made an appointment on the spot. One month later, tests revealed Debbie had a small cancerous tumour hidden in her bowel.

'While it's many years since that day, I shudder to think what might have happened had I ignored my butterfly feelings,' said Debbie.

When I read for people I often experience their emotions, aches or pains. Departed loved ones too will use psychic feelings to identify themselves by creating physical sensations in my body. For example, if a departed loved one has passed from a heart attack I'm likely to feel heaviness or pain around my heart – physical symptoms that instantly vanish the moment I correctly interpret the psychic information being sent to me. Of course, not all psychic feelings are unpleasant.

Once, during a reading, I had two women in Spirit coming through simultaneously – one slightly older than the other. I asked that they give me more information so I could identify them for my client.

'Oh my goodness,' I said to my client, 'I feel like I've just eaten the most amazingly rich and moist chocolate cake.'

My client laughed and said, 'Well, that's definitely my grandmother. Her chocolate cake was a show-stopper.'

The amazing thing is once I've correctly interpreted the psychic feeling signals I receive, the symptoms or sensations instantly vanish – which can be very disappointing when a chocolate cake is involved.

Psychic hearing

Have you ever been humming a song in your head only to switch on the radio and hear the exact same song? When that happens to me, I'm usually synchronised to within one or two words. Perhaps you've run to answer the phone only to discover it wasn't actually ringing – until you turn to walk away.

People who tune into psychic hearing signals are not limited to detecting sound within the physical world. Many people report hearing noises, warnings, fragments of music or snippets of words that defy all logical explanation.

Not so long ago I literally bumped into a bright and bubbly young woman at a Sydney café. Before I could apologise she chirped rather loudly, 'You're the psychic from *The Morning Show*.'

I smiled and, before I could reply, 'Hi, I'm Mitchell,' the woman introduced herself as Taylor and said, 'You'll never believe what happened to me yesterday.'

Undies, undies, undies

Late for work, yet busting to go to the bathroom, Taylor jumped off at her city stop and ran into the train-station toilets. Minutes later she exited the toilets much relieved, but quite late for work. So Taylor decided to power-walk her way through the jostling crowds of suited workers. But all the time she was dodging this one and darting around that one, a voice inside Taylor's head kept saying, *Undies, undies, undies*.

When Taylor entered her office building and squeezed into an already crowded elevator she noticed a few people chuckled. Taylor looked around but couldn't see the source of their amusement. Again the voice inside her head said, *Undies, undies, undies.* Again she ignored it. Seconds later, Taylor felt a tap on her left shoulder. She turned around. A kind, older woman wearing a cleaner's uniform whispered, 'Love, you've got your skirt tucked up in your undies.'

Everyone in the lift burst out laughing.

'Mitchell, I learnt a very valuable lesson,' laughed Taylor.

'Let me guess,' I said. 'Always listen to the voice within.'

People who pick up psychic hearing signals can hear information from the Spirit World. They often say things like, 'I thought I heard …' or ask, 'Did you hear that noise?' And typically, no one else heard a thing. It's much like when a dog hears a dog whistle, yet the noise is silent to human ears.

Year of the dog

Just recently Dr Ross, a prominent veterinary surgeon, walked into my office carrying a jade carving in her hand. She looked worried.

'Although there is nothing unpleasant about the appearance of this carving,' said Dr Ross, waving it as she spoke, 'I think it might be cursed.'

Now it was my turn to look alarmed. 'Why would you think that?' I asked.

'Because it's making me hear things no one else can,' replied Dr Ross.

She placed the jade carving on my desk and I could see that it had a rather striking stylised design. She told me it was a gift from her elderly neighbour who had recently returned from visiting his extended family in China.

'A night or two after I placed this carving on my bedside table,' said Dr Ross, 'I suddenly woke up at two in the morning positive I could hear a dog barking in my room.'

Yet when Dr Ross turned on her bedside

light, the barking mysteriously stopped. But seconds later, her mobile phone rang. It was her elderly neighbour asking for help. He'd woken up in pain and was home alone.

A few days later, on a quiet Sunday morning, Dr Ross was sitting at the breakfast table reading when she heard the soft paws of a dog padding its way down the stairs behind her. 'I could even hear its toenails clicking on my polished floorboards,' she said. 'But when I turned to look, there was no dog there – and the noises vanished.'

But when turning her head in the direction of the noise, Dr Ross caught sight of her elderly neighbour through her living room window. He'd just fallen over in his garden and was struggling to right himself. She ran outside to help him.

'One week later I woke again at two in the morning to the sound of a dog frantically barking at my front door,' said Dr Ross. 'Without hesitation, I got out of bed, slipped on my dressing gown and ran to the front door ready to rescue the troubled animal.'

But when Dr Ross carefully opened her front door, she jumped back in shock. Collapsed on the porch was her elderly neighbour. She immediately checked his vital signs, rolled him into the recovery position and dialled for an ambulance.

'Nothing like this has ever happened to me before,' said Dr Ross. 'Is it possible the carving is cursed?'

'If anything, the jade carving is more like a good luck charm for your elderly neighbour,' I said. 'It seems to have chosen you as its angelic foot soldier.'

I gave Dr Ross other examples of the miraculous ways in which Spirit works. I also explained that when Spirit needs to get our attention they will use whatever means possible. And in Dr Ross's case, Spirit chose to send the sound of a barking dog through to her psychic antenna because they knew it was a sound she'd respond to without question.

'What better way to get a vet's attention?' I said. 'Spirit knew you'd respond without delay and each time they were able to draw your attention in time to help your elderly neighbour.'

Psychic seeing

Have you ever caught a glimpse of movement out of the corner of your eye, but when you turn no one is there? Perhaps you see coloured mists or flashes of darting light as you sense the presence of a departed loved one. Or maybe you start your sentences with 'I see ...' For example, 'I can *see* that if you don't buy a document wallet, you'll lose your passport while travelling.'

People who tune into psychic seeing signals are often known as the family oracle. They continue to surprise and amaze friends by predicting events, or the outcomes of relationships, jobs and holidays days, weeks, months or even years ahead.

A few years ago, Rebecca, a friend of mine, had a dreadful snow-skiing accident while on holidays in Europe. Her abdominal injuries were so serious doctors said it was unlikely she would ever conceive – or if she did, she'd never carry a baby to full term. Even though I predicted she'd eventually have a family, she'd given up trying ... until, one day, her own vision reignited her hope.

'I couldn't believe it, Mitchell,' squealed an excited Rebecca over the phone. 'I was sitting with my friend while she was nursing her newborn baby girl when my vision went hot white and I suddenly saw *myself* nursing a newborn boy – *and* he had the most amazing crop of black hair.'

Two years later, Rebecca fell pregnant and gave birth to her vision – a bouncing baby boy with an amazing crop of black hair.

For Rebecca, and many more like her, Spirit

has a dazzling way of slipping messages to them via their psychic antenna.

A breakfast kiss

Janice was the new girl working in Linda's office. Although they'd just met, their personalities immediately 'clicked', so when Janice invited Linda to her all-night movie marathon, Linda gladly accepted.

But by two in the morning, Linda had slumped down into the soft couch and could barely keep her eyes open.

'I was drifting in and out of sleep when – as clear as day – a vision of an older woman wearing a soft white cotton blouse with delicate yellow flowers entered my mind,' explained Linda.

'Did she say anything?' I asked.

'No,' said Linda. 'She just smiled, blew me a kiss and then vanished.'

The next morning Linda woke early and wandered into the kitchen. Janice's mother,

Mavis, was just sliding a tray of ham and cheese filled croissants into the oven. Linda introduced herself.

'Mavis was so sweet,' said Linda. 'She invited me to share a freshly brewed coffee with her.'

As Mavis and Linda sipped their coffee, Mavis reminisced about how she used to rise early and sit with her mother chatting in the kitchen.

'I don't know what made me think of it,' said Linda, 'but I suddenly interrupted Mavis and asked if her mother ever wore a soft white cotton blouse with yellow flowers on it.'

Mavis raced out of the kitchen and returned minutes later clutching a photograph. As Mavis handed the frame to Linda she said, '*This* is my mother. She loved this photo because she's wearing her favourite blouse.'

'Mitchell, I couldn't believe my eyes,' said Linda. 'Mavis's mother was wearing a soft white cotton blouse with yellow flowers on it

– just like the woman I thought I saw standing in Janice's lounge room the night before.'

Then, for no reason at all, Linda felt compelled to blow Mavis a kiss from across the breakfast table – just as the woman in her vision had done.

Tears welled up in Mavis's eyes. Linda grinned. Mavis put down her coffee and gave Linda a big hug.

'Thank you,' she said. 'My mother used to blow me a kiss like that every morning from across the breakfast table.'

As I later explained to Linda, sometimes we receive messages intended for others because our psychic antenna is open and able to receive.

Linda's story reminds me of another client of mine, Michael. Living a lifestyle as fast paced as the magazine he works for, Michael rarely stops to reflect on life. His mind is always busy. If he's not thinking about new ways to sell fashion then he's occupied with entertaining friends and keeping fit. But not so long ago, Spirit slipped Michael a message – a friendly wake-up call. The experience was so out of the ordinary, Michael booked a reading with me.

Toasting the simple things

'I was on my way to work and stopped to fill my Porsche with petrol,' explained Michael. 'As vapours wafted up from the tank I turned my head to escape them, but in doing so, a woman sitting in the car at the pump opposite me caught my attention.'

Michael described the woman as regal looking with grey hair. But there was also something very odd about her – he couldn't quite put his finger on what it was.

At first Michael thought it was the woman's unflinching, upright posture that made her look unusual. 'But as I continued to study her,' he said, 'I realised she was dressed like Queen Victoria *and* that she was holding an antique tea cup.'

When the owner of the car returned, Michael watched him open the door and ease himself into the driver's seat. Not once did he glance at the regal-looking woman sitting next to him.

'It was so surreal,' said Michael. 'The woman sat with her tea cup as if frozen in time.'

But when the car began to pull away, Michael saw the woman snap into life. She turned ever so slightly. A faint smile crept across her face before she toasted Michael with her tea cup, as if to say 'bottoms up'.

'That's when I realised I could see straight through her,' said Michael. 'I think I saw a ghost!'

I have no doubt Michael saw a ghost – as he put it – but his vision was much more. The regal-looking woman was a message from Spirit. Michael was being told to slow down and enjoy the simple things in life – like a cup of tea.

Psychic dreaming

Has the future ever flashed before your eyes in a dream? Perhaps you've had a visitation from a departed loved one who delivered a reassuring or profound message. While psychic dreams provide remarkable glimpses into the future, they can also be wonderful windows into the Spirit World – occurring only when the mind is relaxed, open and receptive to psychic dream signals.

The majority of our dreams are just dreams – a review of the day's events, thoughts and ideas. But some dreams tap into our fears – bringing to our attention our deepest and most worrying concerns. A psychic dream, on the other hand, is unmistakable because it is 'stand-out' different. The theme is clear, the images vivid, and thoughts so unforgettable that the dream lingers in your mind for hours or days afterwards.

Workshop students often remark that the

people and places in their psychic dreams seem so *real* they're convinced they're experiencing the events first hand. While others recall psychic dreams in astounding detail, some students are instead left in awe of the crystal clear imagery and amazing colours.

When any dream lingers or presents with a recurring theme, it is definitely one to pay attention to. I sense that resting within lingering or memorable dreams are loving messages from departed loved ones, divine guidance, prophecies or even warnings about events yet to unfold – as Karen discovered.

Caught out

Six years ago Karen owned a half share in a very successful hairdressing salon. Blessed with natural style, Karen also had unbridled talent that made her the fashion queen when it came to cut and colour trends. But one night, a dream turned her world upside down.

'I dreamt my business folded,' said Karen.

'I saw myself closing the doors and crying. But the odd thing was, Mum came to visit just before it all happened.'

When Karen confided in Adele, her business partner, that she dreamt their salon would close, Adele laughed.

'It's my job to worry about the business side of the salon. Your job is to focus on what you do best.'

Yet despite Adele's reassurances, Karen's dream kept repeating itself.

'If it wasn't me closing the doors on the salon and crying,' explained Karen, 'an official-looking man wearing a suit would snatch the salon keys off me, or I'd open the cash register and all the money would fly out, or I'd turn around to see all my clients' hair had fallen out.'

For six months Karen's dream-theme persisted. Then one day, Adele rang in sick. Karen was run off her feet. Between cutting and styling hair Karen was managing her staff, answering phones, and dealing with stock deliveries.

'I looked up and saw Mum walk into the salon,' said Karen. 'I was so happy to see her, but in the same instant I felt sick. My dreams suddenly flooded back to me.'

Karen's mum had just returned from a caravanning holiday. She was shocked to see how much weight Karen had lost. Karen confessed that a recurring dream had been playing on her mind.

'Sweetheart,' said Karen's mother, after listening intently. 'Those dreams are all about money and your business.'

Karen smiled and patiently explained to her mother that Adele said the business was in good shape financially. 'But, Mitchell, as I soon as I said that I realised I had trusted Adele with all the banking and finances.'

The knot that had been in Karen's stomach for months suddenly tightened so hard she almost fainted. Karen immediately ran to the telephone. Her dreams had started to make sense.

'I rang my accountant,' said Karen. 'I cried when he informed me that my business owed the tax department over seventy thousand dollars and that none of the staff's superannuation had been paid for over twelve months.'

Adele, Karen later discovered, had been embezzling the salon's profits. Instead of paying taxes and superannuation she'd hidden the money in a personal bank account. But thanks to her psychic dreams, Karen caught Adele out. She pressed charges and saved her business from closing.

Sometimes there can be several elements to a psychic dream. These elements are much like pieces in a jigsaw puzzle – with the picture only becoming clear and the meaning fully comprehensible once all the pieces are joined together.

While some elements within a dream can be very literal, others can be so symbolic that their meaning is temporarily hidden. Not so long ago, I met a lovely woman who said she had long been confused by a sweet little purple bird that flitted in and out of her dreams. She knew the little bird was significant because it would softly whistle the most beautiful lullaby. But she was never sure of its exact meaning. So I suggested she start a dream diary.

Curiously, time revealed that the appearance of the sweet little bird in her dreams coincided with wonderful news in her waking day that someone close to her was pregnant.

When it comes to decoding and clarifying dream symbols, dream dictionaries can prove a useful *guide.* But keep in mind that not all dream symbols have a universal meaning. For example, an apple to one person may represent good health, but to another it may represent bitterness – much like the poison apple in the fairy tale *Snow White.*

Over the years I've encouraged clients and workshop students to keep a dream diary – with many discovering that their dream diary evolves into their very own unique dictionary of symbols, personalised understandings and interpretations.

While flicking back through the pages of my own dream diary I now realise that every time I see falling autumn leaves, my dream is warning me change is coming. In addition to symbolic messages, psychic dreams can also have packaged within them visitations from departed loved ones – as Leander discovered.

Dreams that glitter

Thirty-two-year-old Leander had been in a relationship for five years when she and her partner agreed it was time to start a family.

'I fell pregnant almost immediately,' said Leander. 'But at twelve weeks my partner woke up one morning and said, "I can't do this any more." '

Abandoned and pregnant, Leander felt like her life had been ripped out from under her feet. She was devastated. Night after night she cried herself to sleep. 'I felt so bad. All my life

I'd dreamt of raising a happy family and there I was pregnant, alone and flooding my unborn baby's world with tears.'

Then one night a seemingly ordinary dream marked the beginning of a remarkable turnaround for Leander.

'In the dream I could see myself clearly. I was seven months pregnant, without a partner, and I looked like a beached whale,' said Leander. 'I had received an invitation to a thirty-fifth birthday party.'

Leander recalled not wanting to go to the party because she didn't know the birthday girl all that well, but at that very moment her departed mother appeared.

Represented by a loving presence glowing white with angelic light, Leander's departed mother gently took Leander's hand and guided her forward.

'A kind-faced man with a warm, caring smile stepped forward from the crowd,' recalled Leander. 'He handed me a silver envelope.'

Leander looked at the envelope, saying, 'But I'm not the birthday girl.' The man answered, 'I know, but *I* am here for *you*.'

'When I slid out the card and opened it, the words immediately dissolved into sparkling gold glitter that danced around my pregnant tummy,' explained Leander.

At that moment, Leander's departed mother reappeared. She smiled and said, 'I love you, Leander. Everything will be all right now.'

Several months later, on a bright sunny morning, Leander was flicking through her mail when she spotted a silver envelope.

'I couldn't believe it,' said Leander. 'I opened the silver envelope. Inside was an invitation to a thirty-fifth birthday party.'

When Leander opened the invitation, gold glitter fluttered out and sprinkled itself all over her seven-months-pregnant tummy.

Curiously, upon arriving at the actual birthday party, Leander was greeted by an older woman wearing a simple white dress.

'She took my hand and guided me toward the party guests,' said Leander. 'And the first person she introduced me to was Todd – a lovely man with a warm, caring smile.'

Leander couldn't help but feel there was something very familiar about Todd.

'I was just about to ask Todd if we'd met before when I heard myself think, *Oh my goodness! He's the man from my dream.*'

Todd and Leander married twelve months later. And I'm thrilled to say that at the time of writing this chapter, Spirit whispered Leander was about to fall pregnant with Todd's child.

Just as we can receive psychic dreams during sleep, the same is true for our waking hours. In the brief moments our concentration drifts or our mind slips into autopilot, all sorts of profound psychic signals can reach our psychic 'daydream' antenna.

'While I was cycling to work one morning,' said Mark, a computer programmer, 'my mind drifted off. The next thing I knew, lines of computer code were scrolling so fast in front of my eyes I couldn't read it. Then all of a sudden the scrolling stopped. And there, highlighted in blue text, was a string of code I didn't recognise.'

Only once Mark arrived at work did he realise his daydream had shown him the solution to a programming problem he'd spent the last two days trying to resolve.

Cindy, forty-four, is a busy mum with three young children.

'One morning I was waiting for my youngest to tie her shoelaces. While I was focused on the shoelaces my mind drifted,' explained Cindy. 'In that split second I saw my daughter's right shoelace come undone and then I heard her crying.'

Cindy didn't think any more of it and hurried her daughter along. But just after lunch that day, Cindy received a call from her daughter's school. Cindy's daughter had fallen over and badly grazed her knee.

Once, I was with a film crew shooting a segment for Channel 7's *The Morning Show* at Sydney's old Quarantine Station – reputedly one of Australia's most 'haunted' historic sites. The group touring with me were absolutely amazed by the psychic signals they were picking up on. Some felt cold touches and sensed the residual heaviness of despair. Others said their hands tingled. Many felt cold chills run down their spine and even noticed sudden and inexplicable temperature changes in certain areas. But one man in the group said, 'I think my psychic antenna must be broken.' Compared to the others in the group, he didn't appear to be picking up on any psychic signals. But as I explained to the gentleman, some people tune into signals better than others.

I also find that some people set their expectations too high and by doing so they block their own ability to detect the signals. Plus, not everyone's antenna will receive signals in the same way.

For some people, a psychic signal can be coming through loud and strong. For others the very same signal is faint and weak. So much depends on the person, place, time and circumstances.

So when you next see a fleeting glimpse out of the corner of your eye, feel your hands tingle or the hairs on the back of your neck rise, feel 'good' or 'bad' energy in a room, hear a voice within offer guidance or advice, see the future, experience an 'ah-ha' moment in the shower, daydream a solution, or meet a departed loved one in a dream – trust that you are receiving psychic signals via your psychic antenna. All that might be needed is a little finetuning.

CHAPTER 7

PSYCHIC PROTECTION

Britney's jaw dropped. The tall, refined woman strutting toward her was none other than Rachel, her number one arch rival from high school days.

'Mitchell, at the mere sight of Rachel fear shimmied down my spine, goosebumps prickled my skin, and my stomach twisted itself into a tight knot,' said Britney.

'I heard you'd started this tiny hairdressing business,' Britney recalled Rachel saying with an air of superiority. 'Of course I now own three high-class salons in Melbourne.'

Not trusting herself to speak, Britney grimaced slightly and smiled. But while walking Rachel over to the wash basins, Britney felt oddly light-headed.

'It had been ten years since I'd last seen Rachel,' confessed Britney, 'but being near her made me feel hollow and empty – just like I did years ago at school.'

As Britney applied shampoo to Rachel's wet hair, she did her best to put aside unresolved feelings from the past. But the minute Britney began massaging the shampoo into Rachel's hair and scalp, her energy was instantly zapped away.

'It felt like Rachel's hair had just sucked my very life force out of me,' said Britney.

Britney's knees weakened. She began to wobble on her feet. The apprentice raced over and steadied her before walking her toward a seat at the back of the salon.

Whenever we encounter negative energy it drains us. Perhaps like Britney you can recall a time when you felt tired, drained or zapped after being in the company of a friend, relative or co-worker.

Maybe you even experienced a sudden mood change or felt dizzy, light-headed or spaced-out. There is an invisible thread of psychic energy that links us to those we relate to on a daily basis. Just like air, psychic energy is an unseen force. Its effects can be positive or toxic and negative.

I recall another client of mine, Beverly. She works in an office where the competition is fierce and the air is so thick with rivalry, you can carve it.

Just after lunch one day Beverly was walking toward her office when a sharp pain stabbed at her back.

'The pain was so intense I actually turned around expecting to see someone standing behind me holding a knife,' said Beverly.

Instead, when Beverly turned to face forward

again, one of her colleagues was standing in front of her.

'You're back – finally,' snapped the woman. 'The boss wants to see you. He's really angry. You didn't hand in your report *before* going to lunch.'

'But you said you'd hand in my report with yours,' said Beverly.

'Really?' said the woman, with a smirk. 'I don't recall ever saying that.'

Psychic attack

I remember a story my Nanna Lucy once told me. During her younger years she was sitting on a tram heading home from work. She hadn't been on the tram long before an uncomfortable feeling started to creep over her. When my nanna looked up to investigate where the feeling was coming from, she met the piercing stare of an old woman seated just in front of her.

The old woman's stare was so intense that my nanna found it hard to look away. Nanna said her eyes instantly began to burn and she felt as if the old woman were throwing spears of dark energy at her.

By the time Nanna arrived home, she had an excruciating headache accompanied by inexplicable nausea. Nanna's mother (my great-grandmother Josephine) sat her down and asked what was wrong. When Nanna recited the encounter with the old woman on the tram, my great-grandmother explained to her she'd come under psychic attack. As soon as my great-grandmother cleared the old woman's dark cloud of energy from my nanna's aura, she instantly felt better.

'Next time when you feel someone glaring at you in a bad way,' Nanna Lucy recalled my great-grandmother saying, 'only look at their left eye.'

My great-grandmother Josephine believed

doing so broke the link of negative energies being exchanged.

While my nanna's psychic attack was certainly intentional, most are not. I recall a lovely client named Laura. She was what I call a 'go-to' person. At work, if anyone had a problem or didn't know how to do a task, Laura was there to help. Laura's girlfriends all confided in her. Whether they had relationship troubles, financial issues or simple daily stresses, Laura was there to offer comfort and solve problems. So it wasn't any surprise when Laura said, 'Mitchell, I feel exhausted. I'm mentally and emotionally drained and I don't know why.'

Laura had become what I call a 'psychic sponge'. She was unintentionally absorbing the problems, feelings and worries of all those around her. And while many people left Laura feeling much better – Laura herself was left feeling exhausted and drained.

Just as people can unintentionally drain

our energy, so too can certain locations and buildings.

A friend of mine once worked for a technology company. During a period of rapid expansion it became clear there was not enough office space to house new staff. So the director asked my friend to investigate a vacant government building located directly across the road from their existing office block.

The instant my friend entered the old 1940s building with the real-estate agent, chills ran down her spine.

'It was as if sadness and fear oozed from the walls like sap from a tree,' explained my friend. 'I felt weighed down, dense and heavy.'

Noticing my friend's initial reaction, the real-estate agent mentioned the building had quite a dark and sad history. I sense that's why the building had remained vacant for years.

Many people intuitively sense 'good' or 'bad' energy – especially when walking into a room or meeting someone for the first time.

Whenever I sense negativity in a room I usually walk out again – where possible, I avoid negative energy attaching to me.

Haunted houses

Hauntings can happen anywhere, at any time, and in any building – old or new. Much depends upon the history of the land, the location of the foundations, the former occupants and any lingering residual energies. That's why I say homes not only have a past, but they also have an 'energetic' history.

Many dramas unfold within a home. Arguments are voiced, babies are born and birthdays are celebrated. Departed loved ones are mourned, marriages planned and family and friends welcomed. And as the occupants come and go over time, they each leave behind fragments of their stories and energy.

Residual energies and powerful emotions – especially those stemming from a sudden tragic event – can imprint themselves onto the very walls and foundations of a home or building. Sometimes, residual energy can lay dormant for years, decades or even centuries until just the right circumstances present themselves. Then, when they do, the resulting activity is often completely bewildering to the occupants.

Out of the blue, I received a telephone call to help a teenage girl named Kayla. A ghostly figure had suddenly started appearing in her bedroom.

At precisely one o'clock most mornings, the air in Kayla's bedroom would fill with the crisp scent of Estée Lauder's White Linen perfume. Shortly after that, a beautiful, ghostly bride would step out from Kayla's bedroom wall, walk across the room, and then disappear. Kayla tried speaking to the bride but she went about her business as if Kayla wasn't there. On one occasion the bride walked through Kayla. Not once during her appearances did the bride turn her head or speak. She just floated elegantly across the room as if rehearsing for her walk down the aisle.

Despite the bewildering and regular encounters, I sensed Kayla was not in danger. What she was witnessing was not a spirit haunting her, but rather a residual energy haunting.

Thirty years ago a young bride – not much older than Kayla – dressed for her wedding day in Kayla's room. Tragically, the young bride was killed in a car accident on the way to the church. She never got to walk down the aisle. Kayla was simply experiencing the leftover memories and emotions that had imprinted themselves onto the very walls of her bedroom.

Just as a replay of residual energy can be mistaken for a truc haunting – so too can friendly visits from the Spirit World.

Some years ago a husband and wife came to me for a reading. I can still recall the fear etched into their voices. A terrifying presence was menacing their home – and, in particular, their five-year-old daughter, Zoe.

'Most nights we hear a bloodcurdling scream followed by Zoe yelling, "The man with a stick is standing over my bed,"' explained Zoe's mother.

When Zoe's parents rushed into her room and switched on the light, Zoe was usually frozen stiff with fear.

'I cried when Zoe pleaded with me to move to Nanny's because she didn't have a ghost with a stick living in her house,' said Zoe's mother.

As the ghostly encounters continued, Zoe became so scared she refused to sleep at night. So her parents were left with no option but to invite Nanny to stay over and sleep in Zoe's room.

All was quiet the first two nights Nanny slept in Zoe's room. But on the third night, Zoe let out another bloodcurdling scream and then shouted, 'Look out, Nanny! That man with the stick is after you too.'

I can't tell you how worn down Zoe's parents looked when they trudged into my office that day. But as soon as they finished recounting their story, I sensed the presence of an elderly gentleman coming through.

I didn't mean to scare them, he communicated in a sudden gush. *I just wanted my little Zoe to know I'm always on duty keeping her safe.*

The 'man with the stick' was none other than little Zoe's departed grandfather. He was appearing in full police uniform. The 'stick' was the baton secured to his belt. Zoe's grandfather served on the police force all his working life. And even though he was in Spirit, he still felt it was his duty to protect his loved ones.

Confusing a friendly Spirit visitation with a haunting is an easy mistake to make. And while truly chilling hauntings are usually rare, they have been known to occur.

Several years ago I was contacted by a lovely young couple, Mal and Jacky. They'd just bought a beautiful, modern farmhouse for an unbelievably low price. But within weeks of moving in, Mal and Jacky discovered why the house had been so cheap – it was haunted.

All homes creak and groan. For some people it takes a few weeks to get used to the sounds of a new dwelling – especially at night. But Mal and Jacky were never going to get used to the sound of screaming echoing from the bedroom they were using as a home office.

'The first night it happened,' said Jacky, 'I woke up screaming "The house is on fire!"'

'I thought Jacky was just having a night-mare,' added Mal. 'But then I smelt something burning too.'

'The smell was so vile,' said Jacky, 'we both ran outside dry retching.'

'But once we were outside,' said Mal, 'we realised the house wasn't on fire.'

'There wasn't even a puff of smoke coming out of our chimney,' added Jacky.

From that night forward Mal and Jacky were regularly woken by phantom screaming and a vile flesh-burning smell. During the day,

Jacky complained she felt like she was burning up with fever whenever she tried to work in the study.

'Nothing could quench my thirst or cool me down,' she explained.

As Mal and Jacky sat in my office recounting their story, I suddenly sensed a very dark presence – one I felt was the cause of their problems. I sensed the presence was male, strong, calculating and malicious. I immediately created a super shield of protection in my mind – preventing the dark presence from advancing any further, but I could still sense it simply didn't want Mal or Jacky anywhere near its home.

I quickly explained how dark energies feed off fear – emphasising how important it was for Jacky and Mal to stay calm and fearless. Additionally I armed them with specific tools of protection to cleanse their home of this troublesome spirit.

Days later, Jacky phoned me; as I'd asked,

she'd done some research. I was intrigued to learn Mal and Jacky's home was built over of the foundations of an old farmhouse – one with a very dark 'energetic' past.

After suffering years of violence at the hand of her farmer-husband, the last occupant of the former homestead finally filed for divorce. The farmer was so enraged, he tied his wife to a kitchen chair and set fire to the house. But as he stood watching the burning flames lick at his screaming wife, a heavy wooden beam crashed through the ceiling and pinned him to the floor. Both the farmer and his wife died as their house burnt down to the ground. How dark. How tragic.

Every home, building and location has an energetic past. That's why it's important to spiritually cleanse or apply psychic protection before taking up residence anywhere new.

Several months before I wrote this chapter, Becky came to me for a reading. She also expressed grave concerns about a rental home she and her family had just moved into.

'Mitchell, I think the house is plagued with misfortune and is making us sick,' said Becky. Intuitively, Becky sensed something was odd about the house, but she couldn't put her finger on what. 'The house was clean and well presented,' she said. 'The layout and design suited us perfectly.'

Despite the house prickling her skin, Becky knew it was too good to refuse just because she felt something odd. Yet, two weeks after moving in, misfortune rained down on Becky and her family like a tropical storm.

'I instantly went from feeling energetic to constantly drained, tired and irritable,' she told me. 'A good night's sleep was just a distant memory.'

Becky also noticed she was shouting at her children – something she never did. In turn, her normally delightful and happy children were increasingly uptight, anxious and uncharacteristically argumentative. Even Becky's husband couldn't escape the torrential downpour of misfortune. Two days after moving in, he was retrenched from a job he'd worked at for five years.

As Becky continued to list all the things that were suddenly going wrong in her life – Spirit flashed images of her home through my mind's eye.

'Is your house located in a cul-de-sac at the bottom of a hill?' I asked.

'Yes,' said Becky, astonished.

'When you open the front door, do you look out and up at all the other houses in the street?'

'Yes,' replied Becky.

Immediately, I knew the major cause of Becky's problems. 'When you moved in,' I said, 'did you apply protection?'

'I made sure the house had security lights and an alarm system – if that's what you mean,' answered Becky.

Just as we shield ourselves from unseen forces

so too can our homes benefit from psychic protection and regular spiritual cleansing. In Becky's case, all the negative energy leaking from the homes above her was flowing down the hill like a river. And the natural pooling point was at the bottom of the cul-de-sac – right at Becky's front door.

I suggested Becky place black tourmaline crystals by her front door. Black tourmaline is known for its protective qualities. I also explained how important it was for Becky to cleanse her crystals weekly by holding them under running water.

Negative energy – just like dust and dirt – can accumulate inside a home – particularly in corners, crevices and unused spaces. So I also explained to Becky how to cleanse her home by burning sage.

Native American Indians have long burnt sage believing the sacred smoke dispels negative energy and clears troublesome spirits. Sage smudge sticks can be bought online or at most new-age speciality stores. If you haven't seen one before, a sage smudge stick looks like a bundle of dried leaves bound together with a string.

Using a sage stick is simple. And as Becky discovered, once you have the sage stick producing a healthy plume of smoke you simply enter each room and wave the sage stick in a circular motion.

When I sage my home, I use my free hand to waft the sage smoke into corners, cupboards and stairwells – any place where negative energy can linger or accumulate. Be sure when cleansing your home with sage smoke to leave windows and doors open. That way fresh clean air can rush in to restore a positive balance.

Saging is extremely effective and powerful when it comes to spiritually cleansing a home of negative energy or protecting yourself against psychic attack. I regularly circle sage smoke around my body, my reading room and the inside of my home for this very reason. How you use it is up to you:

I've always been able to sense if a home gives off good or bad energy, wrote one real-estate agent. *After attending your workshop I now carry a sage stick with me every time I go to inspect a new listing – just in case I need to spiritually cleanse it.*

Another woman wrote: *I always sage myself after visiting my mother-in-law's home. Her heart is in the right place, but boy, can she bring you down with her negative conversation.*

A German photographer, who was on assignment in Australia to photograph the Red Centre and Uluru in particular, couldn't thank me enough.

Out of desperation, he searched the internet for an Australian psychic and just happened to be guided to me. He asked if I knew why his vehicle was plagued with so many mysterious breakdowns while travelling in outback Australia.

Sensing the problem, I explained it was important he cleanse his vehicle after visiting each remote photographic location. I felt sure that in some of the places he was visiting the spirits of the land were ancient and deep. Honouring their presence was as important as respecting the customs and traditions of the indigenous peoples of any land.

Thereafter, the photographer experienced no further mechanical problems. He returned to Germany with stunning photographs of Australia's magnificent Red Centre.

Tools of protection

The tools of psychic protection I use and share with you here are easy and flexible. They can be adapted to suit your beliefs and lifestyle. For me, safeguarding my aura has become second nature, just like washing my hands before dinner.

Keep in mind you're not limited to using one

technique at a time. You can mix and match until you develop a technique that suits your specific psychic protection needs.

Bubble of light

Before I leave home for the day, I spend five minutes protecting myself with purple and gold light – my favourite colours. I close my eyes and draw in a few deep breaths to still my mind. In my mind's eye, I imagine my body surrounded by a bubble filled with purple and gold light. You can use whatever colour appeals to you but ensure the light extends over the top of your head and under the soles of your feet.

Next, I slowly exhale. As air leaves my lungs I imagine the purple and gold light forming a super shield – empowering my aura with the ability to deflect all negative energy. To close my bubble of light I thank Spirit for sending me divine protection.

Whenever you feel added protection is needed, do what I do. Dab a drop of lavender oil on the back of your neck. The neck is one of the first places psychic attack occurs. Anytime you sense negative energy, or you know you're going to be in the company of energy zappers or dumpers, reapply lavender oil.

Sea salt

Is there a room that drains your energy? Perhaps it's a family room or bedroom at home, or your office at work. If so, I recommend placing two tablespoons of sea-salt crystals in each corner of the room. Then, once a week for three weeks, vacuum the old salt piles and replace them with fresh sea-salt crystals.

Feng shui experts have long suggested sea-salt crystals exposed to the air naturally attract and absorb negative energy. Be sure to empty the vacuum cleaner every time and dispose of the old salt in an outside garbage bin.

Folded arms and crossed legs

Have you ever suddenly felt like you've come under attack from an unseen force? Perhaps you entered a room, were seated at a family gathering or in a meeting at work. You might even have been in the middle of a telephone conversation.

Whenever you suddenly feel tired, hollow or drained, simply fold your arms over your abdomen and cross your legs to shield your energy. Alternatively, you can place your hands over your abdomen and cross your legs. And, when possible, angle your body away from the source of negativity.

Psychic shielding

Sometimes we find ourselves in situations where we have to address an unpleasant situation, collaborate with uncooperative team members, or negotiate with particularly difficult people. I sense that during these times it is important to psychically shield yourself behind a wall of protection.

I prepare for confronting or draining situations by standing with my hands stretched above my head. At the same time I visualise pushing a layer of protective energy upward as I affirm to myself, 'Protection to the sky.' I then push my arms toward the ground and affirm, 'Protection to the earth.' I then push out with both arms and affirm to myself, 'Protection to my sides, front and back.' I finish by visualising the powerful wall of protection I've just placed around myself.

Door guardian

Just as we can benefit from shielding ourselves with a psychic wall of protection, so too can we shield our work space by creating a door guardian.

In your mind's eye, visualise fixing to the doorway an invisible golden screen. If you work in an open-plan office, simply visualise placing a golden screen around your desk. Affirm to yourself, 'Negative energies shall not enter my space today.' As you go about your day, don't be surprised if you find some people keep their distance, while others walk straight up to you.

Mirrors

There may be times when you need additional help protecting your energy from the people around you. This might be especially so when you're surrounded by complainers, pessimists, energy dumpers, or negative energy flowing from your neighbours.

All you have to do is picture yourself in the centre of a ring of mirrors. With the reflective side facing out, the mirrors will deflect any negative energy being directed at you.

Recently, a client of mine was so distressed by her neighbours' loud, angry arguments she developed severe tension headaches. So I suggested she place a very small mirror above any doors or windows facing the troublesome side.

Mirrors have the effect of turning unwanted negative energy away from your home. As I said to my client, don't be surprised if your neighbours even pack up and move away.

CHAPTER 8

TUNING IN: SEEKING PSYCHIC GUIDANCE

Have you ever found yourself wishing you could see into the future? Or maybe you've pondered a very difficult question, longing for an answer. Perhaps you've heard yourself asking, 'Am I on the right path?'; 'What does the future hold for my children?'; or 'When will my finances improve?'

When searching for answers to compelling life questions like these, psychic guidance can offer valuable insight – especially when you're looking for specific direction or seeking specific solutions. Sometimes psychic guidance even turns up unannounced.

Josh and April were so excited. They'd heard so much about Portugal's Algarve Gypsy Markets. The place was alive with colour and brimming with locals and tourists. Wicker, wood, ceramics, fabrics, clothes and souvenirs burst from the stalls while the heavenly aroma of exotic food made for a delicious sensory experience.

'Mister,' said a heavily accented Portuguese voice.

Josh turned sharply. A very old woman wearing a silk scarf, seated at a stall, made eye contact with him. She motioned for Josh to take something clasped in her weathered hand.

'Misfortune,' she said, pressing what Josh thought felt like a necklace into the palm of his hand. 'This will save you from death.'

'How much?' asked Josh, smiling at the old woman's crafty attempt to sell her jewellery.

Yet to his amazement, she shook her head, refused his money and waved him away.

'Mitchell, the sorrow reflected in her eyes scared me,' explained Josh, retelling the story many months later.

When Josh opened his hand, lying on his palm was a crystal pendulum, not a necklace.

'Come on,' said April, peeking over Josh's shoulder to inspect the pendulum, 'we're in the land of gypsies – let's ask it if we should go scuba diving tomorrow.'

Moments before the old woman caught Josh's attention, April had just said she felt the dive operator's equipment was old and might not be safe.

Ordinarily Josh would have laughed off April's concerns, but this time he didn't. He handed the pendulum to April. They sat down under a shady tree. April fished out the information brochure the dive operator had given them and held the pendulum over it.

'Should we go scuba diving tomorrow?' asked April.

The pendulum hesitated then swung a very definite 'no'.

'See – I told you so,' said April, making her point by playfully poking Josh in the ribs. 'Will Josh meet "misfortune", like the old gypsy woman warned?'

'Mitchell,' said Josh, recalling the moment clearly. 'I felt my stomach drop. The pendulum swung "yes".'

All that night Josh tossed and turned – the old woman's sorrowful eyes haunting him awake.

After a restless night's sleep, Josh woke before dawn. Unable to shake his feeling of unease, he gently woke April. 'I think we'll change our dive plan.'

April rubbed her sleepy eyes and tried to focus on her boyfriend.

'Something doesn't feel right,' continued

Josh. 'We'll do the shallower 25-metre dive and skip the forty-metre one.'

April agreed.

Several hours later, the dive boat slowed to a stop and dropped anchor. Josh and April, kitted out in scuba-diving gear, plunged off the side of the dive boat and descended into the crystal clear blue ocean below.

'I was at twenty-five metres, just drifting along watching the colourful fish, when I suddenly had a sense something was wrong,' said Josh. 'In the next instant the hose attached to my tank burst – immediately cutting me off from the air I needed to breathe.'

With only the air remaining in his lungs to keep him alive, Josh knew he had precious few seconds left to save himself. Survival instincts kicked in. Josh dumped his weight belt and finned as hard as he could. He knew that even if he did make the 25-metre swim to the surface, he'd probably die from a burst lung, an embolism, or the bends.

When Josh next opened his eyes he was encased in a huge steel barrel. At first he thought he was dead, but quickly realised he was in a decompression chamber.

'Mitchell,' said Josh, 'had I stuck to our original dive plan, I wouldn't be here today.'

While most of us will never encounter such a close call with death, Josh's experiences highlight that we can all tune in and seek guidance about the past, present and future.

Pendulums

Pendulums have a long and fascinating history that reaches back over thousands of years. In ancient times villagers used pendulums to locate life-saving drinking water. Colonial miners used them to discover valuable oil and mineral deposits hidden well below the earth's crust.

Even today, some psychic detectives use pendulums to find lost children and runaway pets. Others use them with great accuracy to forecast the future or pinpoint illness in the human body. I know many home healers who use them to locate trouble spots and negative energy vortexes in homes.

I have a friend who consults her pendulum whenever she needs to make important decisions. A client of mine says her pendulum helps her unmask the true feelings of others. In fact, pendulums can be used to make choices of any kind, answer yes/no questions, find missing objects, and offer guidance concerning the past, present and future.

A pendulum is simply a weight suspended from a chain or string. While most pendulums sold in metaphysical bookshops and new-age stores can be made from gold, brass, wood or crystal, you could try making your own simply by suspending a ring, pendant, or crystal from a chain or string.

One particular year when I was holidaying on Queensland's Gold Coast, I felt compelled to walk into a jewellery store. As I scanned the display cabinets the reason I'd been guided into that particular store became clear. Sitting inside one of the display cabinets was an exquisite handcrafted amethyst and moonstone pendulum attached to a sterling silver chain.

Selecting a pendulum is a very personal experience. I sense pendulums should be chosen as you would select a crystal, precious gemstone or any other psychic tool. Hold the pendulum in your hand. How does it feel? Often what resonates with one person may not with another. So while I adore my amethyst and moonstone pendulum, you may very well find yourself drawn to a pendulum made from brass or wood.

When using a pendulum for the first time, be sure to define its directional swing for answering yes or no. To do this simply hold the pendulum's chain between your thumb and forefinger – but make sure the narrow end of the pendulum is not touching anything and that it is free to swing. Next, focus your mind and tune in by asking the pendulum to indicate which direction signals 'yes' and which 'no'.

Alternatively, you could define the directional swing of your pendulum by asking questions you know have a true 'yes' or 'no' value. For example, 'Is my name Mitchell?'; 'Is my favourite colour purple?'; or 'Am I an only child?' Note in which direction your pendulum swings in response to each question.

In my case, my pendulum always motions in a straight line for 'yes' and a circular clockwise direction for 'no'. Your pendulum may respond differently.

On occasions I sometimes find my pendulum swings in a different direction – one that signals neither 'yes' nor 'no'. Should this happen, it often means your pendulum is indicating 'maybe' or that perhaps you're not meant to know the answer at this time. Sometimes it is Spirit's way of saying, 'All will be revealed in divine time.'

Recently, during one of my psychic development workshops, Jasmine had a puzzled look on her face.

'Mitchell, I'm having trouble getting my pendulum to respond to my questions,' said Jasmine.

As I walked toward Jasmine, I could see she was holding the pendulum's chain between her thumb and index finger. She had even supported her elbow on the table like I'd shown her. But I sensed Jasmine's body was too stiff. She wasn't relaxed. And by not being relaxed, she was unintentionally blocking her ability to tune into her question.

'Jasmine,' I said, in a calm, soothing voice. 'Relax your body – open your mind to the flow of energy around you – and then seek clarity with your question.'

Moments later, from across the other side of the room, I heard Jasmine exclaim, 'Oh my goodness – it works. It really works!'

Jasmine's story reminds me of a dear friend

of mine. Not so long ago, she was miserable. To everyone else, her boss was charismatic and charming. Yet, when backs were turned he was mean and very manipulative. My friend just knew he was the reason she'd missed out on several promotions.

After professional workplace counselling failed to improve the situation, my friend decided it was time to leave and find a new job.

'Mitchell,' she said, one sunny lunchtime, 'I've been offered a new position with another company.'

'Are you going to accept?' I asked, genuinely excited.

'I'm not too sure – something doesn't feel right,' answered my friend. 'So I've asked for another day to consider the job offer.'

'Perhaps you could consult your pendulum for further guidance and validation,' I suggested. 'You're about to make a very important decision.'

So before returning to the office my friend

sat on a park bench, removed her wedding ring and suspended it from a gold chain she usually wears around her neck. Holding the ring over her open palm my friend asked, 'Should I accept this new job offer?'

Much to my friend's astonishment, the ring indicated 'no'. When she asked, 'Should I keep my current job?' the ring swung 'yes'.

After finishing work that day my friend rang me again. 'Mitchell, what possible benefit could there be for me staying with my current job? I'm *miserable*!'

'Perhaps the future has bigger plans for you than you have for yourself,' I suggested.

Just after ten o'clock the next morning my friend rang once again. 'Call me crazy,' she said, 'but I turned down the new job offer.'

All was revealed several weeks later. When my friend rang she was squealing with delight. 'My boss has been transferred – to another state!' she exclaimed. 'And guess who landed his job? *Me!*'

Perhaps you're like my friend and have a pressing question concerning your career options. Maybe your question is about a relationship, the fidelity of a new lover, a property, or a situation concerning a child at school.

Sometimes when my clients have concerns relating to affairs of the heart, family members or business partners – and they've brought to the reading a related photograph, personal item or object – I hold my pendulum over the item. I then tune in and ask for answers in relation to their questions. You could try this too.

Just recently, Sandy, who attended one of my psychic development workshops, lost her passport while exploring the ruins of Pompeii.

'We'd just spent three hours exploring the ruins,' said Sandy. 'My husband and I were sitting in the café enjoying a refreshing cup of tea when something made me check I still had my passport in my handbag.'

Much to Sandy's horror, her passport had

fallen out somewhere within the ruins of Pompeii.

'My husband was panicking,' said Sandy. 'And the idea of retracing three hours' worth of our steps made me want to cry.'

But then Sandy remembered back to my psychic development workshop where I'd said that a pendulum is simply a weight suspended from a chain or string.

Quick as a flash, Sandy whipped the wet teabag out of her cup and squeezed the remaining liquid into the saucer. She then opened her map of Pompeii and laid it flat on the table. Using the teabag like a pendulum she held it over each area printed on the map and asked, 'Is this where I dropped my passport?'

'My husband was so embarrassed,' said Sandy. 'But after five "no's" the teabag finally swung "yes" when I held it over the area marked *The Temple of Apollo*.'

Rushing straight to the Temple of Apollo with her husband, Sandy found her passport

– just as her pendulum had indicated. No one had noticed it because the dark blue cover was partially obscured in a blue-grey shadow.

Playing cards

Just like pendulums, playing cards have long been used to predict the future and forecast the outcome of things to come. Similar to tarot cards, those who consult playing cards find they reveal just as many hidden messages, predictions and prophecies. For instance, the fifty-two playing cards correlate with the weeks of the year. The twelve court cards (kings, queens and jacks) represent the twelve months of the year or significant people in your life. The four suits often signify the four seasons or the elements – earth, air, fire and water.

My great-grandmother Josephine used to read playing cards all the time. If she was reading for a man, she'd draw the king of hearts from the pack and place it face up on the table. If it was a woman, she'd select the queen of hearts. Next, she'd shuffle the cards, cut the deck and shuffle the two halves back into each other.

Using a cross spread, she'd place three cards to the left of the single card she'd drawn. Cards to the left signified what was coming in from the future. Then she'd place three cards to the right, which signified what was leaving that person's life. She'd also place three cards at the top, which signified what was on the person's mind; and another three cards at the bottom, which signified all the elements the person needed to kick away – like risks, vulnerability and jealous or negative people. Then she'd place three cards in the centre, over the top of the original card, which signified what the person was holding in their heart.

For my great-grandmother, Josephine, hearts represented spring and corresponded to the element of water. They signified love, friendship, happiness and domestic concerns. 'Hearts,' she used to say, 'are happy cards.'

Clubs represented summer and corresponded to the element of fire. They signified business, ambition and achievement. They generally indicated success and happiness.

Diamonds represented autumn and corresponded to the element of earth. They signified career and money issues.

Spades represented winter and corresponded to the element of air. They signified gossip, bad tidings and challenges. Generally they indicate upsets.

Like my great-grandmother, Josephine, I also find the ten of diamonds represents successful tidings with money and finance – which is a wonderful card to receive. And whenever an ace turns up in my readings it signifies new beginnings and opportunities. Whenever a jack and queen turn up together, they represent a married couple.

Understanding playing-card spreads and

unravelling the predictions and prophecies hidden within them – like my great-grandmother once did – takes time and much dedication. Thankfully there are many well-written books that explain how to interpret the in-depth and intriguing meanings encoded into each playing card. But there are also simple ways to tune in with playing cards, ask questions, and receive immediate guidance.

Find yourself a quiet spot – somewhere you won't be disturbed. Remember to switch your phone to silent. Take a few deep, cleansing breaths. Shuffle the playing cards and focus on your question. Divide the deck of cards into three piles and then shuffle them back into each other. Keeping the cards face down, fan the deck out across a table or flat surface. Close your eyes and, using your non-writing hand, pass your palm over the fanned-out cards. Does your hand feel drawn toward some cards and not others?

One at a time, select three cards you feel

most drawn to. Place each one face down on the table. Open your eyes. One at a time, turn each card over, noting its colour.

In answer to your question, *three* red cards represent a *strong* 'yes' while *two* red cards indicate 'maybe'.

Three black cards, on the other hand, reveal a *strong* 'no'. While *two* black cards indicate 'maybe'.

If you find 'maybe' is a frequent answer to a particular question – it may mean the decision is still in the balance and that it could swing either way depending on events yet to unfold. So keep in mind nothing is ever set in stone. The decisions we make today can affect the outcomes of tomorrow.

Several years ago, Aimee, one of my students, couldn't choose between two men vying for her attention. Hayden was handsome, charming, successful and full of life. And while Adam was good looking, he was the quieter and more studious type.

Given several of Aimee's friends were also swooning over Hayden, they decided my workshop was the perfect place for Aimee to ask for guidance in relation to affairs of her heart. So even though Aimee secretly sensed Adam was a better choice, she shuffled the playing cards and asked, 'Should I start a relationship with Hayden?'

Aimee drew the seven of spades (black), the nine of clubs (black), and the three of clubs (black) – a very definite *no*!

Pleased the cards had said 'no' to Hayden, Aimee started dating Adam with confidence. Meanwhile, one of her friends started dating Hayden.

Six months later, Aimee ran into her friend and asked how she and Hayden were getting along.

'Fantastic,' replied Aimee's friend, 'until I caught him cheating on me with *three* other women!'

Aimee was flabbergasted. And while she

felt sorry for her friend she also thanked her lucky cards that she'd tuned in and trusted the guidance she'd received.

Psychic gym

When joining a gym for the first time, no one instantly bench presses fifty kilos or leaps straight into an advanced Pump class. The same is true when beginning to develop and strengthen your psychic muscle.

There are many simple and accessible exercises you can do at home to develop and strengthen your psychic muscle. Take your telephone for instance. When it rings – tune in and see if you can sense the gender of the caller before you answer. Note how many times you are correct. Before preparing the evening meal – focus on one particular family member. Visualise their smiling face. Tune into their thoughts and ask yourself what would they like for dinner?

When approaching your letterbox – tune in. In your mind's eye visualise how many envelopes are waiting to be opened. What colour are they? How many will be bills, letters, or parcel delivery notes? When driving your car, envisage where you'll find a parking space. One of my all-time favourite psychic strengthening exercises is forecasting which line at the supermarket check-outs will move fastest.

Over time, by regularly practising these simple psychic strengthening exercises, you will intensify your ability to tune into psychic energies – which for some can lead to the gift of psychic healing.

CHAPTER 9

PSYCHIC HEALING

The instant Ted arrives home from work Margaret can immediately sense whether her husband has a tension headache.

'He doesn't need to say a word,' said Margaret the day I met her. 'I simply motion for Ted to sit on the massage chair I keep in the kitchen.'

Margaret then dabs her secret blend of remedy oils on Ted's temples and asks him to calm his mind and relax.

'What I think is amazing,' said Ted, 'is how my wife's hands heat up after she places them on either side of my forehead.'

'Once my hands are warm and my fingers begin to tingle,' continued Margaret, 'I know it's time to begin massaging Ted's temples, neck and shoulders.'

'My wife's hands are better than any hot pack,' said Ted, proudly. 'I tell everyone she can siphon away headaches with her fingers.'

'It's nothing special,' said Margaret, blushing, 'but a lot of people do come to me to shift their headaches.'

Have you, like Margaret, ever reached out and found your touch has healed someone? Perhaps you have given a much-needed hug and added sunshine to someone's day. Maybe you kissed a skinned knee and put a smile on a child's face. Many people have a magic touch when it comes to soothing a crying baby. I even know some whose contact helps small children spring back to health, vanquishing colds and fevers in half the time.

For centuries, healers have used their hands and various other methods of natural healing to cure the sick, clear energy blockages and restore balance to the human body. Remarkably, many of these natural practices are still in use today with great effect.

In the November 2010 issue of *That's Life* magazine, my healing hands touched readers Australia-wide with astonishing results.

In the article entitled 'Let these hands help you', readers were asked to lay their hands on top of a photograph of my palms – either at the scheduled times or when they felt the need. I, in turn, sat in deep meditation at the listed times. Calling upon universal healing energy, I visualised projecting blue healing light outward through my hands. In my mind's eye, I saw the blue light reaching many hands and giving healing where needed most.

The feedback was remarkable. Some readers reported feeling 'lighter' and 'happier' after placing their hands on my mine. And for one reader, the result was profound:

When I first touched Mitchell's hands on the

page, wrote Sharon, *I felt a warm tingling sensation and then I saw a blue gardenia, which turned into a blue light and then transformed into a lotus. I felt a strong jolt in my body and then my hands felt like they were being pulled through the page. This happened five times before I finally came back to reality! Following the healing I felt very calm and happy – like I was on a cloud.*

The initial shift Sharon experienced had such a profound effect on her emotional well-being she repeated the healing. The second time around, however, the result was *life changing.*

I no longer feel the need to rely on drinking every night to get me through, wrote Sharon, *and my depression seems to have lifted. Thank you so much, Mitchell, for all your spiritual help.*

Sharon's letter was humbling. Her openness touched my heart and resonated deep within my soul. If, like Sharon, you'd like to try using my healing hands, visit my website (www.

mitchellcoombes.com) to print a copy of 'Let these hands help you'.

Healing thought patterns

Just as our hands can aid healing so too can our words, thoughts and beliefs.

Months ago, Chris, a forty-year-old man, came to me for a reading. As he moved across the room to sit down I could already sense why he had booked in to see me. In my mind's eye a string of doctors, physiotherapists and chiropractors flashed past. All of them were puzzled – unable to diagnose the cause of Chris's debilitating back pain. While I'm not a general practitioner and I don't give medical advice, I immediately sensed Chris's back pain was not medically related but rather 'energetic' – symptomatic of his emotions.

Chris had reached a point where he no longer felt supported – no one 'had his back' any more. Particularly lonely since his recent divorce, Chris felt he was carrying the weight of the world on his shoulders.

I explained to Chris that pain and discomfort in the body – without any direct medical or physical cause – is often a manifestation of the words we speak, the thoughts we think and the beliefs we hold deep within our being. Sadly, if these negative thoughts are not addressed, the mind's *dis-ease* can quickly turn into the body's *disease*.

Naturally, Chris was concerned when he realised that his own words, thoughts and beliefs were the likely causes of his back pain.

'That's interesting,' said Chris, 'I often complain I feel unsupported.'

Chris had almost resigned himself to believing back pain was a permanent part of his life and that he'd feel alone and unsupported forever. Yet, all Chris needed was to choose his thoughts carefully, be mindful of the words he spoke and weed out any negative beliefs he held deep within. So instead of complaining,

'I'm alone and unsupported' Chris needed to think positively and verbalise thoughts such as 'I am loved and supported by life'.

Just as the reading was ending, Chris's departed father came through. The sense of love and support he radiated was enough to fill many hearts, not just Chris's. When I told Chris his departed father was right by his side guiding and supporting him, he dropped his chin to his chest as whispered a prayer-like, 'Thank you.'

Three weeks later, Chris rang me – his voice light-hearted and happy. He didn't need to tell me his back pain had vanished: I had already sensed it. Chris was pain free and in a much more positive and happy place.

Chris reminds me of other clients. As one young woman sat on the chair opposite me shuffling the tarot cards she complained her left hand was sore.

The left hand is often associated with issues of receiving. I sensed my client found it hard to accept compliments, help from others, and healing – but she wasn't alone.

Another woman had a slightly more mysterious problem with her left hand. Without warning she'd lose sensation in her fingers and drop whatever she was holding. In my mind's eye, I could see she had let significant career opportunities slip through her fingers because deep down she felt unworthy of success.

As I explained to the first client, her sore left hand was a sign she'd been turning away the help others had offered in return for all the kindness she'd shown them. The second client was losing her grip as a sign she needed to work on her confidence and affirm within herself that she was worthy of success.

Unusual or sudden problems with one or both eyes can be a sign there is a problem with your universal vision. Ask yourself, 'What is going on in my life that I'm not seeing?' A similar thing applies for the ears. Ask yourself,

'What am I not hearing?' Could it be you're missing an important message from Spirit?

Sudden pain or stiffness in the neck can also be a message. For instance, my friend began waking up with a painful neck lock. Blaming her mattress and pillow, she spent a small fortune buying new ones. Had she spoken to me first, I would have asked, 'Who – or what – is the pain in your neck?' As it turns out, my friend's neck problems coincided with the day her boss moved her to the customer complaints department. Neck pain or stiffness is often a sign certain stresses in our lives need addressing.

Curious problems with the throat can also be a tell-tale sign that feelings have been suppressed and emotions like anger and hurt have been swallowed.

I once knew of a woman in her mid-fifties who had frequented the same bus stop for years. One day her personality changed from outgoing to withdrawn and silently bitter.

Whenever someone new arrived at the bus stop, she would strike up a conversation and unload her tragic story onto them. Each time her story would end with the same three phrases: 'He broke my heart'; 'I'm never going to get over it'; and 'I'll take the pain to my grave'.

Eighteen months later, the woman collapsed at the bus stop and died from a heart attack – taking with her the pain she had so often mentioned.

Just as many of the clients I've read for have discovered, we all need to choose our thoughts carefully, be mindful of the words we speak and weed out any negative beliefs we hold deep within.

Tools of healing

While there are many gifted energy healers, massage therapists and natural therapy practitioners to call upon, the tools of healing I use and share here are for use at home. But as wonderfully simple as these tools are, they are not meant to replace treatment recommended by trained medical professionals. Instead, you can use them to complement any other treatment you may be receiving.

Healing hands

Hold your hands up and study them for a moment. Did you realise hands are the most powerful natural healing tools known to humankind? For centuries, healers have used the laying on of hands to restore health.

Today, massage and reflexology are the most popular of thc centuries-old touch-based healing systems. And just like the healers of old, modern massage and reflexology therapists understand how the body's organs and glands correspond to particular areas on the ears, feet and hands. By simply applying pressure, they know how to relieve sore muscles, relax a stressed mind and restore balance to the body's natural immune system.

You too can tap into the healing power of your own hands. Simply close your eyes and relax your breathing. Silently request to receive healing where it is needed most. Now gently rub your hands together to open yourself to healing vibrations. Gently place your healing hands on the areas of your body where healing is needed.

While your hands are resting on your body, take notice of any sensations you experience. Your hands may begin to tingle or become incredibly warm. Perhaps you can detect uncharacteristic cold patches on your skin. Many people report their hands actually feel heavier when located on an area that needs healing. Others say their hands feel lighter when the healing is complete. Some even experience a pulling sensation – as if a mysterious magnetic force is guiding their hand toward the area that needs healing. Even if you don't feel any of these sensations, be reassured healing will always be active – especially if you've set the highest and purest of intentions.

When it comes to reaching out to heal a loved one, or even a pet, follow the same steps as above except lay your hands on your loved one's shoulders. Alternatively, you can try placing one hand on your loved one's upper back and the other on the forehead.

For a pet, try placing one hand near their head and the other on their abdomen. Alternatively, place your hands on your pet's body in whatever position offers them the most comfort and reassurance.

Hold your healing hands in place until you sense the healing is complete. For most people, intuition tells them when to stop or move to another part of the body.

Not so long ago I was in the middle of a reading for a woman when a delightfully fluffy cat came through from the Spirit World. In my mind's eye, I could see the cat mooching around the woman with all the grace of a Persian, but it walked with a limp.

When I asked the woman whether she owned a very affectionate fluffy cat that walked with a limp, she smiled and said, 'Yes, that's Molly. She passed three weeks ago.'

I sensed my client had spent many hours sending healing to Molly's hip – warming and soothing the joint as much as she could. Molly the cat had simply returned to say thank you to her beloved owner for the kind healing she'd given during the last days of her life.

Molly the cat's story reminds me of a good friend of mine, who is spiritual healer. Her dog regularly sneaks into her healing room and lies on his back under the massage table during a client's treatment. He then closes his eyes and falls asleep. Animals respond to healing vibrations just as much as we do.

Broken-heart therapy

Two years ago, a bright, bubbly and charismatic

young woman named Natalia visited me for a reading. Sadly, a bad relationship had burnt Natalia so badly she confessed she could 'never bring herself to love again'. Yet, during the reading, I sensed the most amazing long-term relationship was just around the corner for her.

When I mentioned the potential of new love, Natalia stared at me open-mouthed then said, 'As wonderful as that sounds, Mitchell, I've locked up my heart and thrown away the key.'

Sadly, Natalia's fear of history repeating itself meant she was pushing opportunities away. She was creating a future of further heartache and loneliness. Hiding her heart behind a solid wall, her love could not get out nor new love reach in.

So for twenty-one days I asked Natalia to dab essential oil of rose over her heart and affirm to herself, 'I open my heart to unconditional love' and 'It *is* safe for me to love again'. At the same time, I asked Natalia to imagine a beautiful pink rose opening over her heart and envisage the sun's glorious rays kissing each petal with loving sunshine.

Two months later, I received an email from an ecstatic Natalia. Spirit had guided her to enrol in a photography class – something that was completely out of her comfort zone. In the process, she had met a wonderful new man who kissed her heart with loving sunshine.

Pyramid healing

Ancient Egyptian records speak extensively about the mystical healing powers of pyramids. Even recent studies have shown that small model pyramids can preserve certain foods for longer, maintain the sharpness of razor blades and energise water. Today many people enjoy the benefits of meditating under pyramid structures.

My Uncle Aram, who was a gifted tarot reader and astrologer, often made pyramid meditation hats out of coloured cardboard. By combining colour with meditation, he could amplify the healing power of his pyramid to help revitalise his energy, balance his thoughts and heal his body.

If you're not as crafty as my uncle was with cardboard, or you don't have the funds spare to buy a model pyramid, try my pyramid visualisation technique.

For a few minutes each day sit somewhere comfortable – preferably in a peaceful place where you won't be disturbed. Clear your mind and calm your breathing. In your mind's eye, visualise yourself sitting under a beautiful pyramid filled with your favourite colour. With the purest of intentions, ask that your pyramid's power reach the areas of your mind, body and life that need energising, healing or balancing.

Flower remedies

When someone is upset or sick we often send them flowers. I sense flowers aren't just about brightening someone's day with perfume and colour; they carry within them hidden and divine healing qualities.

Can you recall a time when the sweet scent of a rose lifted your spirits? Maybe you were strolling through a lavender field and remarked how calm and relaxed you felt afterwards. Perhaps you were crushing peppermint leaves to add to a refreshing summer punch when you inhaled the pure cleansing aroma simply because it felt good.

Tapping into the divine healing qualities of flowers is not a new concept. The ancient Egyptians believed a flower's fragrance came from the gods so mortals could enlighten themselves by absorbing the various aromas.

Centuries ago, healers of old would drape gauze-like cloths over flowers and plants to collect the morning dew – knowing each droplet of precious moisture contained within it the healing qualities of the flowers it had been resting on. Healers would then wrap the flower-infused gauze around the affected body part or wring it out to administer the droplets orally.

Today, flower remedies are readily available as convenient solutions in attractive bottles – just ask at your local health food store. You'll be pleasantly surprised by the variety. There is a flower remedy to heal just about every emotional state. One you may already be familiar with is the five-flower combination Rescue Remedy. Mainly used to relieve feelings of anxiety, nervousness, tension, stress, agitation, or despair, Rescue Remedy provides a sense of focus and calm.

Crystal healing

Special, extraordinary and healing – these properties have been associated with crystals since ancient times. Today, professional crystal therapists report that crystal healing contributes to profound improvements in health and wellbeing.

I find amethyst is a wonderful calming and

healing stone – perfect for dissolving emotional stress.

Rose quartz is another favourite of mine. Besides being a stone of unconditional love and infinite peace, it is the most important crystal for balancing the heart centre. With its ability to purify and open the heart on all levels, rose quartz brings about a deep sense of inner calm, healing and profound self-love. This is an excellent crystal to draw upon when dealing with an emotional crisis.

Clear quartz is a master healer. Admired for its ability to direct and amplify energy, clear quartz can also unblock stagnant energy and infuse the body with healing.

The easiest way to harness the healing power of crystals on a daily basis is to carry them with you – in a pocket or handbag – or wear them as a piece of jewellery. Many people slip their chosen crystal under their pillow at night and ask for healing dreams. I often meditate holding a crystal in each hand.

You may also like to try using crystals for spot healing. Gently massage the affected area using the crystal or simply rest the crystal there. I find massaging in an anti-clockwise direction removes pain while clockwise infuses the body with healing.

When you're using crystals it's important to cleanse them regularly. The simplest method is to wash your crystal under running water. Water neutralises and dissolves any negative energy stored in the crystal. Some people prefer to bathe their crystals in salt water. Others purify them under moonlight – the choice is yours.

By using simple tools of healing on a regular basis, we can introduce a wonderful sense of harmony, self-healing and spiritual wellbeing into our daily lives.

CHAPTER 10

MOST ASKED QUESTIONS

1. How can I help my psychic child?

Mandy, a worried mum, emailed me and asked, *How can I help my psychic child?* If you believe your child has a strong psychic ability, there are excellent books available from libraries and bookstores, plus many valuable online resources. They're all focused on helping you to help children develop their gift.

I am fortunate to have come from a psychic family. My mum understood the mystical ways of Spirit and encouraged the development of my gift. She would often impart wisdom and share spiritual values such as, 'The universe will always provide' and 'Leave it to the capable hands of Spirit'.

You can help by making sure your child's psychic gifts develop in a positive, safe, empowering and loving environment.

Making friends, attending school, completing homework, taking part in family activities, being held responsible for household chores and tending a pet are all equally important skills. Balance is your child's best protection. Above all, keep an open mind and allow your children to come to you with any thoughts, feelings or questions they may have.

2. Can I use my psychic ability to attract my soulmate?

We have many soul connections. Not all of them will be lovers, partners or spouses. Some of our deepest, most treasured and longest relationships will be with a friend, family member, or even a pet. However, I sense the secret to attracting a soul connection partner is radiating and genuinely living the love, honesty, happiness, commitment and special qualities that will make any relationship a happy and rewarding one.

The power of positive attraction is incredible. Why not try it yourself by creating a 'vision card'. Simply take a bright pink piece of card or paper. Place a photograph of yourself in the centre. Thumb through magazines, newspapers and the like. Locate and cut out pictures and words that symbolise the qualities you're looking for in your soul connection partner, but also collect the qualities you intend to *give*. Paste your chosen pictures and words on the card around your photograph. Once you've done that, slip the card under your pillow each night just before you go to sleep. When you wake, go about your day radiating all the qualities you intend to give this person when you meet him or her. Divine timing and synchronicity will do the rest. You'll be amazed.

3. Do departed pets come through in readings?

Absolutely! I have known many departed pets to appear during readings. With tails wagging, coats shining and feathers fluffed, pets charge through from the Spirit World with much enthusiasm. Some arrive with messages while others are simply offering their affection once again.

If you regularly watch Channel 7's *The Morning Show*, you'll know I appear each week to give live readings. Once, while reading for one woman on air, I suddenly sensed a small dog in Spirit around her feet. I felt that when the dog was here on the earth plane it never left her side – they shared an incredible, everlasting bond.

'There is a small dog in Spirit that walks beside you,' I said. At that point the woman raised the hem on her trouser leg. There on her ankle was a tattoo of a small dog – a token of her bond with her much-loved and dearly departed pet.

4. What is a 'development circle'?

Spiritualist churches and psychic groups often hold development circles, which are similar to workshops. Under the guidance of an experienced tutor, members meet regularly to meditate and learn techniques that further develop their psychic intuition. People I've spoken to particularly enjoy learning about meditation, psychic energies, crystals and spirit guides – which are all part and parcel of participating in a development circle. Just keep in mind that if you do attend a development circle of any kind, it's good practice to place psychic protection around yourself before you arrive and to spiritually cleanse yourself of any psychic debris afterwards.

5. What's the difference between a psychic and a medium?

A psychic is able to tune into the past, present and future. They can offer guidance in relation to love, relationships, wealth, health, travel, life path, children and career. A medium, on the other hand, has a direct line to loved ones in the Spirit World. While most mediums are psychic, not all psychics are mediums – I'm the whole package!

6. How can I become closer to my angels and guides?

Your angels and guides love and care about you. Begin working with your team of spiritual helpers by asking for their help and trusting in their divine presence – and by thanking them in advance. When you do, amazing acts of synchronicity, timely messages and spirit-inspired dreams will arrive to help you solve problems and enhance many areas of your life. Getting to know your angels and guides is no different from fostering a new friendship. Through regular meditation – and moments of silence – you can talk to them and ask for help. Be sure to let your friendship unfold and develop naturally. There is no need to know their names or identity at the start. Time will reveal all.

7. What do my experiences of déjà vu mean?

Many people have experienced visiting a place for the first time and feeling as if they have been there before. When meeting someone new many have felt a familiar or inexplicable connection – 'I know you from somewhere' or 'Have we met before?' Sometimes déjà vu experiences are simply 'sign posts' or 'life markers' confirming that you are on the right path. Other times, strong feelings of déjà vu may happen when you are recalling a memory from a previous lifetime.

8. How can you tell the difference between imagination and intuition?

When intuition is at work, you have a very clear, strong and decisive psychic feeling, vision or knowing that compels you to take a particular action, make a particular decision or draw a particular conclusion. There is never a moment of doubt in your mind. The action, decision or conclusion instantly feels right. When imagination is involved, fears are projected and procrastination leaves you feeling doubtful. Always listen to your intuition and trust your first thought or feeling.

9. What does it mean if I keep seeing the same numbers?

Sometimes Spirit will repeat a sequence of numbers in order to deliver a message. Usually these number sequences appear grouped. For example, many people see 1111, 333, 911. These numbers may appear as the time 11.11 a.m., the number on a bus, an address (3/33

Angel Street), or the last digits of a phone number or car licence plate. Each number holds its own special meaning and there is a selection of books and resources on the web available to help you decode the message you're being given. If you've asked Spirit for their help, then when and where these number sequences appear could also be contributing to your answer.

10. Where's the strangest place you've given a reading?

I was thirty thousand feet above the ground, in transit, on a flight between Brisbane and Melbourne while on tour for my first book, *Sensing Spirit.*

After the plane reached altitude, one of the flight attendants asked if I would do a reading for her as she'd recognised me from *The Morning Show.* The flight attendant's departed father appeared next to her – so I said, 'Yes!' I was quickly ushered to the privacy of the crew station – the area where the flight attendants sit for take-off and landing.

And contrary to popular belief, being thirty thousand feet up in the air did not place me 'closer to heaven' – as one passenger so kindly asked upon my return to my seat.

Afterword

A man once dreamt that an angel was giving him a tour of the Spirit World. Together they walked down a long corridor. The man's angel guide stopped in front of a large room, turned to him and said, 'This is the department where requests for divine help and prayers are received.'

The man looked around the room. He could see it was terribly busy. Rows upon rows of angels were sorting thousands of special requests and prayers arriving from earth by the minute.

As they continued walking, they reached a second room. The man's angel guide turned to him and said, 'This is the department where all of the requests for divine help and blessings are lovingly packaged and dispatched for delivery to earth.' Again, the man noticed how busy all the angels were.

Finally, at the farthest end of the long corridor, they stopped at the door of a very small room. To the man's great surprise, only *one* angel sat in the room – idle.

'This is the department of acknowledgment and gratitude,' said the angel guide.

'How is it that there is no work going on here?' asked the man.

The angel guide sighed kindly. 'After people receive their divine help or blessing, very few send back acknowledgment or gratitude.'

As you continue your psychic travels, send thoughts of gratitude to Spirit during your quiet whisperings, meditation and reflective moments. During your day, be an angel – reach out and help others whenever you can.

Acknowledgments

I am truly humbled and blessed by the abundance of kindness, support, and encouragement given to me by so many wonderful people as I journey along my spiritual path. Especially:

My loving family Maria Coombes, Justin Coombes, and Lucia and Lino Marano for your unconditional love, encouragement, support, and devotion.

Robert Reeves, who continues to shine his love and light brightly in my life. I know that our souls are very old friends.

My dear loyal friends, too many to name. Thank you for the beautiful friendships we share. I treasure each and every one of you.

To my wonderful editor Denise Gibb, a true wordsmith and without whom this book would be so much less.

With special appreciation to the entire publishing team at Brio Books, for their continued enthusiasm, support, and for giving my books a new life.

With eternal gratitude to all the readers of my first book Sensing Spirit, and my wonderful clients who've shown me the brilliance of their inner light – may our paths cross again soon.

— Mitchell Coombes

Resources

Books

Browne, Sylvia with Harrison, Lindsay. *Psychic Children: revealing the intuitive gifts and hidden abilities of boys and girls.* Piatkus, UK, 2009.

Browne, Sylvia with Harrison, Lindsay. *The Other Side and back: a psychic's guide to our world and beyond.* New American Library, New York, 2002.

Brown, Sylvia. *All Pets Go to Heaven: the spiritual lives of the animals we love.* Piatkus, London, 2009.

Cheung, Theresa. *Angel Babies: and other amazing true stories.* HarperElement, London, 2009.

Chitty, Dorothy. *An angel set me free: and other incredible true stories of the afterlife.* HarperElement, London, 2009.

Dent, Margaret. *Love never dies: extraordinary accounts of survival beyond death.* Random House, Australia, 1999.

Dosa, David. *Making Rounds with Oscar: the extraordinary gift of an ordinary cat.* Hyperion Books, USA, 2010.

Edward, John. *Infinite Quest: develop your psychic intuition to take charge of your life.* Sterling Ethos, New York, 2010.

Goode, Caron B. *Kids who see ghosts: how to guide them through fear.* Red Wheel/Weiser, San Francisco, 2010.

Hall, Judy. *The Crystal Bible, volume 1: the definitive guide to over 200 crystals.* Octopus Publishing Group, London, 2010.

Hardo, Trutz. *Children Who Have Lived Before: Children from all over the world prove that they have lived before.* Rider Books, London, 2005.

Hay, Louise. *Heal your body: the mental causes for physical illness and the metaphysical ways to overcome them.* Hay House Inc., Australia, 1988.

Newcomb, Jacky. *Angel kids: enchanting stories of true-life guardian angels and 'sixth sense' abilities in children.* Hay House Inc., California, 2009.

Rogers, Rita. *Mysteries: first-hand accounts of the amazing world of the unexplained.* Pan Macmillan, London, 2001.

Sheldrake, Rupert. *Dogs that know when their owners are coming home: and other unexplained powers of animals.* Arrow Books Ltd, UK, 2000.

Smith, Gordon. *The amazing power of animals*, Hay House Inc., New York, 2009.

Van Praagh, James. *Ghosts Among Us: uncovering the truth about the Other Side*. Rider Books, London, 2009.

Van Praagh, James. *Heaven and Earth: making the psychic connection*. Rider Books, London, 2003.

Weiss, Brian L. *Many Lives Many Masters: the true story of a prominent psychiatrist, his young patient and the past-life therapy that changed both their lives*. Piatkus, UK, 2006.

Magazines

Coombes, Mitchell. *Cleanse the negative: the art of protection against psychic attack*. Insight Magazine. Insight Publishing Pty Ltd, April 2006, pg 50.

Online documents

ABC, Catalyst. *Psychic Pets*. 7 April 2005. abc.net.au/catalyst/stories/s1340523.htm

ABC, Science News, *Dogs predict seizures with a sloppy kiss*. 22 June 2004. http://www.abc.net.au/science/articles/2004/06/22/s1137619.htm

BBC. Religion. *The Dalai Lama: the role of the Dalai Lama*. 21

September 2006. www.bbc.co.uk/religion/religions/buddhism/people/dalailama_1.shtml

The Daily Mail. Brennan, Zoe. *Reincarnated: Our son World War II pilot come back to life.* August 2009. http://www.dailymail.co.uk/femail/article-1209795/Reincarnated-Our-son-World-War-II-pilot-come-life.html#ixzz1DceydAoW

Explore Meditation. Ellyard, Karen. *Soulmates.* 2011. http://www.exploremeditation.com/soul-mates/

National Geographic. Mott, Maryanne. *Did Animals Sense Tsunami Was Coming?* 4 January 2005. http://news.nationalgeographic.com/news/2005/01/0104_050104_tsunami_animals.html

Also available by Mitchell Coombes

Do we all have a spirit guide to watch over us? Where do our loved ones go when they die? Can they return to visit and what signs do they send?

Drawing on his remarkable life and experiences, celebrity medium Mitchell Coombes explains what happens when people die – including what happens to children and those who pass tragically. His experiences provide a compelling, reassuring and heart-warming insight into the journey beyond.

Mitchell also reveals how to connect with departed loved ones and the spirit world by helping you to see, hear and sense when they are making contact.

Packed with extraordinary real-life stories of people's touching encounters, you will discover that the Spirit World works in the most amazing, wonderful and life-changing ways.

With Mitchell's exceptional insight and easy-to-follow guidance, you too will be sensing spirit.

9781922598721 (print)
9781925143041 (eBook)

Also available by Mitchell Coombes

The Psychic Soul Oracle Cards by spiritual medium and bestselling author, Mitchell Coombes, offer divine guidance and answers to questions about your love life, career, health, spiritual path and more.

Each of the 44 oracle cards in this unique deck features a beautiful crystal butterfly to help you tune into your intuition and awaken your psychic senses.

With the help of the accompanying guidebook, you'll discover the meaning of each card, the healing qualities of each crystal, and learn how to easily give yourself and others accurate and insightful readings.

9781925143072 (print)